Cybersecurity Exploration: Your Introdu
and Ethical Hacking

Chris Miller

Contents

About this book

In a world where digital landscapes are constantly evolving, the importance of cybersecurity has never been more apparent. As technology advances, so do the methods of potential threats. Amidst this backdrop, *"Cybersecurity Exploration: Your Introduction to Pentesting and Ethical Hacking"* emerges as a comprehensive guide, illuminating the path for those intrigued by the world of ethical hacking and penetration testing.

Imagine embarking on a journey where you not only learn the theories but also gain hands-on experience. This book takes you by the hand and leads you through the intricate labyrinth of ethical hacking, revealing the secrets behind the art of securing systems by understanding vulnerabilities.

Begin your journey by delving into the role of a pentester, learning to differentiate between various hacking approaches. Grasp the essence of the pentesting process, realising that with great power comes great responsibility. Step into the shoes of a defender, a guardian of systems, committed to keeping digital realms safe.

As you progress, discover the building blocks that constitute the foundation of ethical hacking. Unravel the intricacies of networking, TCP/IP fundamentals, and network protocols. Dive into the fascinating world of packet analysis, gaining insights into tools like Wireshark that decipher the invisible streams of data coursing through the digital universe.

But what is a guardian without knowledge? Venture into the realm of information gathering and reconnaissance, uncovering the nuances of passive and active reconnaissance. Explore tools like Nmap and Shodan, harnessing the power of open sources to gather precious data that fortifies your understanding of potential threats.

Your journey intensifies as you learn to scan and assess vulnerabilities. Understand how to identify open ports, wielding tools like Nessus to conduct comprehensive vulnerability scans. Prioritise vulnerabilities for remediation, safeguarding systems against potential exploitation.

Yet, in this world of ethical hacking, the story does not end with identification. The tale continues with exploitation techniques, where you explore the very heart of vulnerabilities. Use Metasploit, the celebrated framework, to delve into exploit development. Craft and launch attacks against vulnerabilities, not to harm but to enlighten, revealing the stark reality of potential breaches.

As you peer deeper, post-exploitation unveils itself as a realm of critical importance. Discover strategies for maintaining control over compromised systems, and gain insights into the art of sustaining access. Here, knowledge empowers you to make systems more resilient, fortified against potential intrusions.

This narrative is not just about technical prowess; it's about ethical responsibility. Throughout your journey, a guiding light reminds you of the significance of ethical conduct. Learn to wield your skills responsibly, staying within legal boundaries, and collaborating with organisations to fortify their defences.

" *Cybersecurity Exploration: Your Introduction to Pentesting and Ethical Hacking*" is more than a book; it's a passport to a realm where knowledge translates into power—the power to secure, protect, and defend. Are you ready to step into this world and become a guardian of digital realms? Your journey awaits.

About the Author:

Chris Miller is an accomplished professional in the realm of cybersecurity, networks, and systems. With a deep-rooted passion for uncovering vulnerabilities and safeguarding digital landscape. He has dedicated his career to safeguarding the digital frontiers through ethical hacking and penetration testing. With a relentless drive to empower the next generation of cybersecurity professionals, Chris stands as a beacon of guidance, bridging the gap between theory and hands-on practice.

As an accomplished lecturer, Chris has navigated the intricate web of cybersecurity with the curiosity of a student and the wisdom of a mentor. His years of experience as a dedicated educator have provided him with a profound understanding of how to translate complex concepts into actionable insights. This ability shines through in his writing, where he unveils the world of ethical hacking and pentesting in a manner that resonates with beginners and junior professionals alike.

Chris's journey began inquisitively, as he embarked on his own quest to understand the dynamics of vulnerabilities, exploits, and defence mechanisms. This journey transformed him into a lecturer known for his engaging teaching style, fuelled by a passion to simplify the seemingly complex. His expertise in the classroom is matched only by his real-world experience as a systems professional, where he has uncovered hidden vulnerabilities, developed defence strategies, and audited networks for organisations seeking robust security.

However, Chris's contributions extend beyond the classroom and boardroom. His insights into the world of pentesting and ethical hacking have become a source of inspiration for those aspiring to enter the field. With an innate ability to empathise with newcomers, he has guided countless students and professionals on the path to ethical hacking mastery.

Within the pages of this book, Chris Miller encapsulates not only his expertise but also his compassion for those embarking on their pentesting journey. He sheds light on the nuances of working as a pentester, illuminating the role's challenges, triumphs, and continuous evolution. For those seeking not only technical proficiency but also a deeper understanding of the cybersecurity landscape, Chris's insights serve as a guiding star, helping readers traverse the exhilarating terrain of ethical hacking and pentesting with confidence and purpose.

Intended Audience: Embarking on a Cybersecurity Odyssey

This book is crafted as a compass to navigate the exhilarating landscape of cybersecurity, designed for individuals who are curious, determined, and eager to explore the realms of ethical hacking and penetration testing. Whether you're a student taking your initial steps into the captivating world of cybersecurity or a seasoned professional seeking to expand your horizons, this book is tailored to offer you a stepping stone into the dynamic universe of digital defence.

Students with Curiosity and Ambition

For the students who are curious and ambitious, this book is a beacon that lights the path to understanding the intricacies of ethical hacking and penetration testing. It is your entry point into deciphering the language of vulnerabilities, exploits, and security measures. With clear explanations, hands-on exercises, and real-world examples, this book equips you with the foundational knowledge needed to embark on a journey of discovery and skill acquisition.

Professionals Eager to Expand Horizons

For the professionals yearning to broaden their skillsets and delve into the world of ethical hacking, this book serves as a launchpad to launch you into uncharted territories. It caters to those who seek to bolster their expertise in cybersecurity, giving you the tools to unearth hidden vulnerabilities, strengthen defences, and contribute to the safeguarding of digital landscapes.

Not a Definitive Guide, but a Guiding Star

It's essential to note that this book is not intended to be a definitive guide to every aspect of ethical hacking and penetration testing. Instead, it is designed as a guiding star— a source of inspiration and knowledge to kindle your passion and lead you toward deeper exploration. It will introduce you to the fundamental concepts, key tools, and essential techniques that lay the groundwork for your journey.

Your Odyssey Begins Here

This book is your passport to an exciting odyssey in cybersecurity. It will empower you to take your first steps, encourage you to ask questions, and inspire you to immerse yourself in a world where curiosity and knowledge intertwine. It invites you to embrace the challenges, the revelations, and the profound satisfaction of uncovering hidden truths in digital domains.

So, whether you're a student setting sail on a voyage of discovery or a professional seeking a new frontier, let this book be your guide as you embark on a cybersecurity odyssey, ready to unravel the mysteries and embrace the opportunities that await.

Chapter 1: Introduction to Ethical Hacking and Pentesting

Welcome to the world of ethical hacking and penetration testing (pentesting)! In this chapter, we'll provide you with a comprehensive introduction to the exciting and challenging field of cybersecurity. As technology continues to advance, the need to safeguard digital assets becomes more critical than ever. Ethical hackers, often referred to as pentesters, play a crucial role in identifying vulnerabilities within systems and applications before malicious hackers can exploit them. Throughout this book, I will refer to Ethical hacking, pentesters and pentesting but all terms are interchangeable and essentially mean the same.

Role of a Pentester: In the ever-evolving landscape of cybersecurity, the role of a pentester is paramount. A pentester, short for penetration tester, is a skilled professional who plays a pivotal role in identifying vulnerabilities within computer systems, networks, applications, and even physical infrastructure. Think of pentesters as the "good guys" who proactively search for weaknesses before malicious actors can exploit them.

Guardians of Security: Pentesters are the guardians of digital security, adopting a proactive approach to protect organisations from cyber threats. Their primary responsibility is to simulate real-world cyberattacks, attempting to breach security defences, just like hackers with malicious intent would. However, pentesters do this with the explicit permission of the organisation they are testing, under controlled conditions.

Ethical Mindset: What distinguishes pentesters from malicious hackers is their ethical mindset. While malicious hackers exploit vulnerabilities for personal gain or harm, pentesters have a strong moral compass. They uphold the principles of legality, ethics, and responsible disclosure. Pentesters aim to uncover vulnerabilities and security gaps not to exploit them, but to provide organisations with the information needed to strengthen their defences.

Proactive Risk Mitigation: Pentesters act as early detectors of potential security threats. By identifying vulnerabilities and weaknesses before attackers can find them, pentesters allow organisations to proactively address these issues, minimising the risk of successful cyberattacks. This proactive approach helps organisations avoid data breaches, financial losses, reputation damage, and legal consequences.

Comprehensive Skill Set: To excel as a pentester, one needs a comprehensive skill set that encompasses various domains of cybersecurity:

- **Technical Expertise:** Pentesters must possess in-depth knowledge of operating systems, networking, web applications, databases, and security protocols.
- **Programming Skills:** Familiarity with programming languages is crucial for developing and modifying exploits, as well as understanding vulnerabilities in code.
- **Analytical Thinking:** Pentesters need to think like hackers, identifying potential attack vectors and devising creative ways to exploit them.

- **Tool Proficiency:** A wide range of tools, such as vulnerability scanners, penetration testing frameworks, and packet analyser's, are essential for conducting tests effectively.

Collaboration and Communication: Pentesters often work closely with various teams, including IT, development, and management. Effective communication skills are essential to articulate technical findings and recommendations to non-technical stakeholders. Pentesters must strike a balance between presenting vulnerabilities in a clear manner and avoiding unnecessary alarm.

Continuous Learning: The world of cybersecurity is ever-changing, with new threats and vulnerabilities emerging regularly. Pentesters must stay up-to-date with the latest techniques, tools, and attack vectors to remain effective in their role. Continuous learning through training, certifications, and engaging with the cybersecurity community is essential for professional growth.

In a rapidly digitising world, pentesters are the unsung heroes who help organisations stay one step ahead of cybercriminals. Their dedication to securing digital assets and maintaining the integrity of systems is invaluable. As you delve into the world of pentesting, remember that your actions have a direct impact on the security of individuals, businesses, and society as a whole.

Differentiating Between Hacking Hats:
1. **Black Hat Hacking:** Black hat hackers are individuals who engage in malicious activities with the intent to breach systems, steal data, disrupt services, and

cause harm. Their actions are illegal and unethical, often resulting in legal consequences.

2. **White Hat Hacking:** White hat hackers are the "good guys." They are ethical hackers who work to secure systems, networks, and applications. Their activities are legal and sanctioned, with the aim of identifying vulnerabilities before malicious actors can exploit them.

3. **Gray Hat Hacking:** Gray hat hackers fall somewhere in between. They might identify vulnerabilities without explicit authorisation but don't have malicious intent. While their actions can be helpful, they often operate in a legal grey area.

Overview of the Pentesting Process: The pentesting process typically involves several stages, each with its own set of tasks and goals:

1. **Planning and Reconnaissance:**
   - Understand the scope and goals of the pentest.
   - Gather information about the target system, network, or application using both passive and active reconnaissance techniques.
   - Identify potential vulnerabilities and entry points.
2. **Scanning and Enumeration:**
   - Conduct scans to identify open ports, services, and potential attack vectors.
   - Enumerate the target to gather information about users, shares, and other resources.
3. **Vulnerability Assessment:**

- o Use tools to assess the target for known vulnerabilities.
- o Analyse the results and prioritise vulnerabilities based on potential impact and exploitability.

4. **Exploitation:**
   - o Develop and execute exploits to take advantage of identified vulnerabilities.
   - o Gain unauthorised access to systems to demonstrate the potential impact of a successful attack.

5. **Post-Exploitation and Lateral Movement:**
   - o Maintain access to compromised systems.
   - o Move laterally within the network to explore further vulnerabilities.

6. **Reporting:**
   - o Document findings, vulnerabilities, and the entire pentesting process.
   - o Create a detailed report with recommended remediation measures for the client or organisation.

7. **Balancing the Realm: The Social, Ethical, and Legal Dimensions of Penetration Testing**

Embarking on the odyssey of penetration testing entails not just mastering the craft of digital exploration, but also grasping the intricate interplay of social, ethical, and legal dimensions. In a world where digital landscapes are intimately connected, your actions as a penetration tester reverberate far beyond lines of code and network nodes. This journey beckons you to navigate the profound responsibility that accompanies your pursuit of knowledge and mastery.

Social Consequences and the Ripple Effect

The realm of cybersecurity is intertwined with human lives and livelihoods. The vulnerabilities you uncover possess the potential to disrupt, expose, and dismantle the digital fabric that organisations and individuals rely on. The consequences of your actions ripple through interconnected networks, impacting not just systems but also the people who depend on them.

Consider the case of a renowned financial institution that engaged in penetration testing to bolster its defences. However, an oversight led to a temporary shutdown of critical services, causing financial strain for customers. This scenario underscores the importance of maintaining open communication, professionalism, and an acute awareness of the broader implications of your actions.

Ethical Integrity: Guardians of Digital Safeguards

Ethics form the cornerstone of your journey into the realm of penetration testing. In wielding the power to expose vulnerabilities, your ethical integrity becomes your guiding light. As you uncover potential exploits, your role as a guardian is to ensure that these revelations are handled with utmost responsibility and empathy.

In an illustrative case study, a healthcare institution contracted penetration testers to assess its systems. The testers, driven by ethical stewardship, unearthed critical vulnerabilities that could expose patient data. By prioritising patient privacy and swiftly alerting the institution, they demonstrated how ethical hacking embodies a commitment to safeguarding the digital welfare of all.

Navigating the Legal Landscape: A Complex Cartography

As you traverse the domain of penetration testing, the legal landscape takes center stage. Each jurisdiction delineates the boundaries within which your digital explorations must unfold. Unauthorised actions, even in pursuit of ethical goals, can result in severe legal repercussions.

Consider a case where a penetration tester inadvertently overstepped legal boundaries and faced legal action. This scenario underscores the necessity of obtaining explicit permissions, adhering to regulations such as the Computer Fraud and Abuse Act (CFAA) in the United States, and respecting the legal frameworks of the regions you operate in.

A Symphony of Responsibility and Mastery

Your journey as a penetration tester resonates beyond the technical prowess you acquire. It is a symphony composed of social awareness, ethical integrity, and legal compliance. Just as a skilled musician combines notes to create harmonious melodies, you harmonise your technical skills with the ethical and legal considerations that underpin your actions.

In your pursuit, consider the case studies that illuminate the complexities of your role. Through the lens of these real-world examples, grasp the symbiotic relationship between your actions, the digital ecosystem, and the lives it touches.

By understanding and embracing the intricate dance of social, ethical, and legal facets, you not only master the art of penetration testing but also elevate it to a form of responsible guardianship in the digital age.

Ethical hacking and pentesting require a strong understanding of technology, an ethical mindset, and continuous learning. As you progress through this book, you'll delve deeper into each stage of the pentesting process, gaining the skills needed to identify, exploit, and mitigate vulnerabilities effectively and responsibly. Remember, your goal as a pentester is to strengthen cybersecurity, protect digital assets, and contribute to a safer digital world.

Chapter 2: Setting Up Your Pentesting Environment

In this chapter, we'll guide you through the process of setting up a robust and isolated pentesting environment. A well-structured environment is crucial for conducting safe and effective penetration tests. We'll cover the installation of a virtualisation platform, creating a virtual lab for testing, and choosing/configuring operating systems.

Installing a Virtualisation Platform:

A virtualisation platform allows you to run multiple virtual machines (VMs) on a single physical machine. This is essential for creating an isolated environment to perform your penetration tests.

1. **Choose a Virtualisation Software:** Opt for popular options like Oracle VirtualBox, VMware Workstation, or VMware Fusion (for Mac users).
2. **Download and Install:** Visit the official website of the chosen virtualisation software, download the installer, and follow the on-screen instructions to install it.

Creating a Virtual Lab for Testing:

1. **Plan Your Lab:** Decide on the number of VMs you'll need for your testing scenarios. Consider having a mix of target systems, attacker systems, and monitoring systems.
2. **Create VMs:** Open your virtualisation software, click "New," and follow the wizard to create new VMs. Install the operating systems you'll use for testing.
3. **Networking Setup:** Configure network settings for your VMs. You can choose NAT for internet access or

create a custom network configuration for more advanced setups.

Choosing and Configuring Operating Systems:
1. **Target Systems:** Select operating systems that are commonly used by organisations. For example, Windows Server, Windows Client, Linux distributions (Ubuntu, CentOS), and other relevant OS versions.
2. **Attacker Systems:** Choose a variety of attacker OS options, including Linux distributions like Kali Linux or Parrot Security OS, which come preloaded with penetration testing tools.
3. **Monitoring Systems:** Include systems for monitoring network traffic and logging activities. You can use a specialised Linux distribution like Security Onion.
4. **Installation:** Install the chosen operating systems on the respective VMs using ISO files or installation images. Follow the installation process, configuring settings like username, password, and networking.

Networking Considerations:
1. **Network Segmentation:** Use virtual network configurations to segregate your VMs. Create separate networks for target, attacker, and monitoring systems.
2. **Network Modes:** Choose network modes such as Bridged (VMs are directly connected to your physical network), NAT (VMs share your host's IP), or Host-Only (isolated network between VMs and the host).

Tips and Considerations:
- Always download software from official sources to avoid malware or security risks.

- Use strong and unique passwords for each VM to prevent unauthorised access.
- Keep your host system and VMs updated with the latest security patches.
- Backup your VMs regularly to prevent data loss.

By following these steps, you'll create a versatile and secure pentesting environment that allows you to safely practice various attack and defence scenarios. Remember, a well-prepared environment is the foundation for successful penetration testing, enabling you to hone your skills and contribute to the realm of ethical hacking.

Setting Up Your Penetration Testing Environment: Step-by-Step

In this step-by-step guide, we will walk you through the process of setting up a basic penetration testing environment using VirtualBox. We'll also allocate IP addresses that will be used in future chapter exercises. This environment will include an attacker machine (Kali Linux), a target machine (Metasploitable 2), and a monitoring machine (Security Onion).

Step 1: Install VirtualBox
1. Download VirtualBox:
   Visit the VirtualBox official website (https://www.virtualbox.org/) and download the installer for your host operating system (Windows, macOS, Linux).
2. Install VirtualBox:
   Run the installer and follow the on-screen instructions to install VirtualBox.

Step 2: Download VM Images
1. Download Kali Linux:

    Visit the Kali Linux downloads page (https://www.kali.org/downloads/) and download the Kali Linux VirtualBox Image (64-bit).

2. Download Metasploitable 2:

    Download the Metasploitable 2 VM image from SourceForge (https://sourceforge.net/projects/metasploitable /files/Metasploitable2/).

Step 3: Create Virtual Machines
1. Launch VirtualBox:
    - Open VirtualBox after installation.
2. Import Kali Linux:
    - Click "File" > "Import Appliance."
    - Select the Kali Linux OVA file you downloaded.
    - Follow the import wizard's instructions, ensuring you allocate sufficient RAM and CPU cores.
3. Import Metasploitable 2:
    - Repeat the import process for the Metasploitable 2 OVA file.

Step 4: Configure Networking
1. Create a Host-Only Network:
    - In VirtualBox, go to "File" > "Host Network Manager."
    - Click "Create" to create a new Host-Only network.

2. Assign IP Addresses:
    Assign static IP addresses to your VMs:
    - Kalı Linux: 192.168.56.101
    - Metasploitable 2: 192.168.56.102
    - Security Onion (later chapter): 192.168.56.103

3. Configure Network Settings:
    - For each VM, select the VM, then go to "Settings" > "Network."
    - Choose the "Adapter 2" tab.
    - Set "Attached to" to "Host-Only Adapter."
    - Choose the Host-Only network you created.

Step 5: Start Your VMs
1. Start Kali Linux:
    - Click "Start" for your Kali Linux VM.
2. Start Metasploitable 2:
    Click "Start" for your Metasploitable 2 VM.

Step 6: Verify Connectivity
1. Verify Kali Linux IP:
    - In Kali Linux, open a terminal and run ifconfig. Ensure it shows the IP address as 192.168.56.101.
2. Verify Metasploitable IP:
    - In Metasploitable 2, open a terminal and run ifconfig. Confirm the IP address as 192.168.56.102.

Now, you have a basic penetration testing environment set up with Kali Linux as your attacker machine and Metasploitable 2 as your target. You can use these IP addresses in future exercises for testing and penetration testing scenarios. Remember to keep your VMs updated and exercise responsible usage of these tools and environments.

Chapter 3: Networking Essentials for Pentesters.

In the world of pentesting, a solid understanding of networking is essential. This tutorial will guide you through TCP/IP fundamentals, navigating network protocols, and using tools like Wireshark for packet analysis. These skills are crucial for identifying vulnerabilities and potential attack vectors within networked systems.

Understanding TCP/IP Fundamentals:

Transmission Control Protocol/Internet Protocol (TCP/IP) is the backbone of modern networking. It's crucial to grasp its basics before delving into pentesting:

IP Addresses and Subnetting: Foundational Concepts in Networking

IP addresses are the foundation of modern networking, serving as the digital identification tags for devices connected to the internet or a local network. In conjunction with subnetting, they enable efficient data routing and organisation within large networks. Let's delve deeper into these concepts with examples to illustrate their importance.

IP Addresses: Uniquely Identifying Devices

IP addresses, whether in IPv4 or IPv6 format, play a vital role in facilitating communication between devices on a network. In IPv4, an IP address is composed of four sets of numbers, known as octets, separated by dots (e.g., 192.168.0.1). Each octet can range from 0 to 255, resulting in a total of over 4 billion possible IPv4 addresses.

Example: Consider a home network with several devices: a computer, a smartphone, and a printer. Each of these devices is assigned a unique IP address to ensure that data packets are accurately directed to the intended recipient. For instance:

- Computer: 192.168.0.10
- Smartphone: 192.168.0.20
- Printer: 192.168.0.30

Subnetting: Efficient Network Organisation

As networks grow in size, managing IP addresses becomes complex. Subnetting addresses this challenge by dividing a larger network into smaller segments, or subnets. Each subnet is allocated a range of IP addresses, allowing for efficient routing, management, and optimisation of network resources.

Example: Imagine a company with multiple departments: Sales, Marketing, and IT. Subnetting allows the network to be segmented for better organisation and security. Each department gets its subnet range:

- Sales: 192.168.1.0/24 (IP range: 192.168.1.1 - 192.168.1.254)
- Marketing: 192.168.2.0/24 (IP range: 192.168.2.1 - 192.168.2.254)
- IT: 192.168.3.0/24 (IP range: 192.168.3.1 - 192.168.3.254)

This separation enhances security and reduces unnecessary network traffic between departments.

Efficient Routing: Subnetting also aids in efficient routing of data packets. Instead of sending data packets across the entire network, routers can determine the destination subnet and forward packets only to the relevant subnet, reducing network congestion and enhancing performance.

Tutorial: Calculating Subnets for IP Address 192.168.0.0/24 with 8 Subnets and 30 Hosts Each

Subnetting is a fundamental skill in networking that enables you to break down a large IP address space into smaller, more manageable subnetworks. In this example, we will calculate subnets for the IP address 192.168.0.0/24 with the goal of creating 8 subnets, each accommodating up to 30 hosts.

Step 1: Understand the Notation

The IP address we are working with is 192.168.0.0/24. The "/24" indicates that the first 24 bits are reserved for the network portion, leaving 8 bits for host addresses within each subnet.

Step 2: Determine the Number of Subnets and Hosts

In this example, we aim to create 8 subnets, each with a maximum of 30 usable host addresses.

- 8 bits for hosts provide $2^8 = 256$ possible addresses.
- Subtract 2 (network and broadcast addresses) to get 254 usable host addresses per subnet.
- We can't have more than 254 hosts, so choosing 30 hosts per subnet is reasonable.

Step 3: Calculate Subnet Masks and Addresses

We need to determine how many bits to borrow for subnetting. Since we need 8 subnets (which requires 3 bits for representation), we will use a subnet mask of /27 for each subnet.

- Convert the original subnet mask /24 to binary: 11111111.11111111.11111111.00000000
- Borrow 3 bits for subnetting, which means the new subnet mask is /27: 11111111.11111111.11111111.11100000

Step 4: Calculate Subnet Addresses

To calculate the subnet addresses, we'll follow these steps:

1. Start with the base address: 192.168.0.0
2. Convert it to binary: 11000000.10101000.00000000.00000000
3. Increment the subnet portion by 32 (binary 00100000), since we're using 3 bits for subnets.
4. Convert the result back to decimal: 192.168.0.32
5. Repeat this process for the other subnets, adding 32 each time.

Step 5: Identify Usable IP Ranges

For each subnet, the usable IP range is as follows:

- Subnet 1 (192.168.0.32/27): Usable range 192.168.0.33 - 192.168.0.62
- Subnet 2 (192.168.0.64/27): Usable range 192.168.0.65 - 192.168.0.94
- ... and so on for the remaining subnets.

Step 6: Document Your Subnets

Document each subnet's network address, usable IP range, and broadcast address. This documentation is essential for configuring devices within each subnet.

In summary, subnetting enables efficient IP address management. By understanding subnetting notation, calculating subnet masks and addresses, and identifying usable IP ranges, you can effectively design and manage subnets to suit your network's requirements.

Subnetting plays a pivotal role in the context of penetration testing, as it offers a powerful means to dissect and analyse complex network architectures. Ethical hackers and penetration testers leverage subnetting to understand the intricate layout of target networks, effectively identify vulnerabilities, and simulate potential attack vectors within specific segments. By subdividing IP address ranges, penetration testers gain granular insights into network subdomains, allowing for precise focus on critical areas that might be susceptible to breaches. Subnetting empowers testers to simulate attacks in controlled environments, isolate vulnerabilities, and ascertain the extent of potential security risks. Ultimately, mastering subnetting equips penetration testers with the ability to navigate labyrinthine networks, fortify defences, and deliver robust recommendations for enhancing overall cybersecurity posture.

Ports and Sockets:

Understanding Ports and Sockets in Networking: Facilitating Communication

In the intricate world of networking, ports and sockets play a pivotal role in enabling seamless communication between devices and applications. Ports allow for the concurrent operation of multiple services on a single device, while sockets provide a means to establish connections through a combination of IP addresses and port numbers. Let's explore these concepts further with real-world examples.

Ports: Enabling Multiplexing and Communication

In the digital realm, a port is like a virtual gateway that allows different applications or services on a single device to communicate simultaneously. Ports are numbered channels that help route data packets to the correct destination within a device.

Example: Imagine your computer as a busy street with various shops (applications) lined up. Each shop has its entrance (port) where customers (data packets) come and go. Common port numbers are standardised for specific services.

For instance:
- Port 80: Web traffic (HTTP)
- Port 443: Secure web traffic (HTTPS)
- Port 22: Secure shell (SSH)

Multiple applications running on your computer can each utilise a different port to communicate independently. This multiplexing capability allows efficient sharing of resources and concurrent operation of various services.

Sockets: The Connection Blueprint

Sockets provide a comprehensive framework for devices to establish connections and communicate with one another. A socket is the combination of an IP address and a port number. When a connection is established, a socket acts as a virtual endpoint through which data packets flow.

Example: Think of a socket as a telephone line connecting two parties. The IP address is like the phone number, indicating the recipient's location, and the port number is like the extension number, indicating the specific service or application within that location. Just as you dial a specific extension to reach a particular person, data packets are directed to the appropriate application using sockets.

For instance, when you visit a website (e.g., http://www.example.com), your device establishes a socket connection to the server's IP address (resolved from the domain name) on port 80. This allows your browser and the web server to exchange data packets seamlessly.

Enabling Efficient Data Exchange

In the context of penetration testing, understanding ports and sockets is essential for identifying potential attack vectors and vulnerabilities. By analysing the usage of specific ports and sockets, pentesters can uncover misconfigurations, exploitable services, and security weaknesses within networks and systems. Moreover, a solid grasp of ports and sockets empowers pentesters to recommend appropriate countermeasures to enhance security and ensure smooth and secure communication between devices and applications.

Here are some examples of common ports and sockets, along with potential ways attackers could exploit them:

Port 80 (HTTP):

Exploit: Attackers could exploit web servers on port 80 by attempting to perform SQL injection, cross-site scripting (XSS), or directory traversal attacks. They might also look for misconfigured servers that leak sensitive information.

Port 443 (HTTPS):

Exploit: Attackers could try to exploit SSL/TLS vulnerabilities, such as Heartbleed, to gain access to encrypted data. They might also set up phishing websites with valid SSL certificates to trick users into divulging sensitive information.

Port 22 (SSH):
Exploit: Attackers may attempt to brute-force SSH passwords or exploit weak SSH key configurations. They might also exploit vulnerabilities in SSH server software to gain unauthorised access to the system.

Port 21 (FTP):

Exploit: Attackers could target FTP servers with weak credentials, attempt to perform command injection attacks through malicious filenames, or exploit vulnerabilities in FTP server software to gain unauthorised access.

Port 25 (SMTP):

Exploit: Attackers might use open SMTP servers for spam distribution, perform email spoofing, or attempt to execute phishing attacks by sending malicious attachments.

Port 53 (DNS):

Exploit: Attackers could exploit misconfigured DNS servers to perform DNS cache poisoning attacks, redirect users to malicious websites, or conduct Distributed Denial of Service (DDoS) attacks.

Port 3306 (MySQL):

Exploit: Attackers might exploit poorly secured MySQL servers to perform SQL injection attacks, gain unauthorised access, or extract sensitive data from databases.

Port 3389 (RDP - Remote Desktop Protocol):

Exploit: Attackers could try to brute-force RDP credentials, exploit known vulnerabilities in RDP implementations (e.g., BlueKeep), or attempt to execute ransomware attacks by gaining access to the system.

Port 139/445 (NetBIOS/SMB):

Exploit: Attackers could exploit vulnerabilities like EternalBlue to spread malware, gain unauthorised access to systems, or perform lateral movement within a network.

Port 67/68 (DHCP):

Exploit: Attackers might attempt to set up rogue DHCP servers to distribute malicious IP configuration settings, leading to man-in-the-middle attacks or network disruptions. It's important to note that the examples provided highlight potential attack vectors, but the effectiveness of these exploits can vary based on factors like system configuration, patch level, and security controls in place. For ethical hackers and penetration testers, understanding these common ports and potential exploits helps them identify vulnerabilities and recommend appropriate countermeasures to strengthen an organisation's security posture.

TCP vs. UDP:
- TCP provides reliable, connection-oriented communication.
- UDP offers faster, connectionless communication but without guarantees.

Understanding the differences between TCP (Transmission Control Protocol) and UDP (User Datagram Protocol) is crucial in a pentest context because it helps you make informed decisions when conducting various types of tests and assessments. Both protocols serve distinct purposes, and knowing when to use each one can greatly impact the effectiveness and accuracy of your penetration testing activities. Here's why understanding TCP vs. UDP is important:

1. Targeted Exploitation:
- TCP: As a connection-oriented protocol, TCP ensures reliable data delivery by establishing a connection and managing acknowledgment of data packets. This makes it suitable for scenarios where data integrity

and reliability are essential, such as web applications or file transfers. Understanding TCP helps when attempting exploitation through protocols like HTTP or SSH, where reliable communication is critical.

- UDP: UDP is connectionless and lacks built-in error-checking and acknowledgment mechanisms. While this makes it less reliable, it's faster and more suitable for scenarios like streaming media or online gaming. In a pentest context, understanding UDP helps when dealing with potential vulnerabilities in protocols like DNS or SNMP, where speed takes precedence over reliability.

2. Vulnerability Analysis:

- TCP: Vulnerabilities in TCP-based protocols often revolve around session management, buffer overflows, and weaknesses in handshake procedures. By understanding TCP, you can better identify and exploit vulnerabilities such as those found in web applications using the OWASP Top Ten list.
- UDP: Vulnerabilities in UDP-based protocols are more likely to involve data manipulation, amplification attacks, or open ports that can be exploited for reflection attacks. Being familiar with UDP helps when analysing protocols like DNS, where attackers may exploit open resolvers to launch DDoS attacks.

3. Port Scanning and Enumeration:

- TCP: TCP port scanning is more reliable due to its connection-oriented nature. Understanding TCP helps when identifying open ports and services on a target system, allowing you to gather valuable information for further exploitation.

- UDP: UDP port scanning can be trickier because of the lack of acknowledgment. Knowing UDP is essential for identifying open UDP ports and services that attackers might use to their advantage.

4. Performance and Efficiency:

- TCP: While reliable, TCP comes with higher overhead due to its connection establishment and acknowledgment mechanisms. In situations where you want to prioritise reliable data delivery, understanding TCP helps you make the right protocol choice.
- UDP: UDP has lower overhead and is suitable for scenarios where speed is crucial, but reliability can be sacrificed to some extent. Understanding UDP helps when dealing with protocols like VoIP or online gaming.

In summary, understanding TCP vs. UDP in a pentest context allows you to tailor your approach to various scenarios. Whether you're conducting targeted exploitation, vulnerability analysis, port scanning, or assessing performance, having a solid grasp of these protocols enables you to make informed decisions that enhance the accuracy and success of your penetration testing activities.

Navigating Network Protocols:

In the realm of cybersecurity, the OSI (Open Systems Interconnection) model emerges as a guiding compass, illuminating the intricate pathways that data traverses within communication systems. It unveils a structured framework, a tiered assembly of seven layers, each entrusted with a distinct role in the orchestration of seamless data transmission. This model, although conceptual, holds profound significance for a pentester—a digital voyager probing the security bastions of networks.

Picture a pentester as an explorer, venturing into the heart of a technological ecosystem. The OSI model unfurls a map before this explorer, delineating the landscape with precision. Each layer represents a realm of functionality, from the tangible hardware at the bottom to the ethereal applications at the top. With this map in hand, the pentester begins to comprehend the flow of data, the interactions, and the vulnerabilities that dwell within.

As our explorer advances, they recognise that each stratum holds secrets and weaknesses. A flaw in the application layer might unravel into a cascade of perilous events that ripple through the transport and network layers. The power of the OSI model lies in this understanding—seeing beyond isolated vulnerabilities to perceive the interconnected vulnerabilities that a malevolent entity might exploit.

With this comprehension, our explorer can tailor their strategies. They arm themselves with tools suited for specific layers, deploying them with precision. An understanding of the OSI model empowers them to dissect complex systems into manageable sections, assessing each layer's security in isolation and as part of a dynamic whole.

But this model extends beyond tactical manoeuvres. It facilitates a common tongue spoken between the pentester and the professionals they collaborate with—administrators, developers, and IT experts. As they converse, the OSI model acts as a lingua franca, ensuring that security concerns are articulated within the context of layers, resonating more profoundly with those who dwell in each stratum.

Yet, perhaps most significantly, the OSI model empowers our explorer to envision the ramifications of their actions. They recognise that an attack at one layer might reverberate through others, cascading into a chaotic symphony of compromised security. This foresight helps them comprehend the extent of potential damage, enabling them to craft mitigation strategies with foresight.

In this symphony of technology and security, the OSI model acts as both a score and a compass. It guides the pentester, ensuring they navigate with finesse and purpose. It aids them in unravelling the complexities, envisioning vulnerabilities, and orchestrating assessments that span the entire spectrum of layers. The OSI model is more than a framework; it's a narrative that enables pentesters to unveil vulnerabilities, enhance defences, and script a tale of secure digital landscapes.

1. **OSI Model Overview:**
   The OSI model defines seven layers (Physical, Data Link, Network, Transport, Session, Presentation, Application) that govern network communication.

2. **Common Network Protocols:**

HTTP, HTTPS, FTP, SSH, Telnet, SMTP, DNS, DHCP, ICMP, and more.

Using Tools like Wireshark for Packet Analysis:

Wireshark is a powerful tool for capturing and analysing network traffic. Here's how to use it effectively:

1. **Installing Wireshark:**
   - Download and install Wireshark from the official website (https://www.wireshark.org/).
2. **Capturing Packets:**
   - Select your network interface and start capturing packets.
   - Apply filters to capture specific traffic, e.g., filter by IP address or port.
3. **Analysing Captured Packets:**
   - Wireshark displays packets in a list with various details.
   - Inspect packet headers to understand source, destination, protocol, and port.
4. **Filtering and Searching:**
   - Use display filters to narrow down results based on specific criteria.
   - Use the search function to find packets containing specific data.
5. **Packet Details and Follow Streams:**
   - Double-click on a packet to view detailed information, including headers and payload.
   - Follow TCP streams to see the entire conversation between two hosts.

6. **Protocol Analysis:**
    - Wireshark can automatically dissect various protocols, making it easier to analyse their behaviour.

Putting It All Together:

1. **Practice Subnetting:**
    - Create a small network and practice assigning IP addresses using different subnet masks.
2. **Capture Real Traffic:**
    - Capture and analyse network traffic on your own local network to gain insights into common protocols.
3. **Identify Anomalies:**
    - Look for unusual patterns in packet captures that might indicate potential security issues.
4. **Hands-On Exercises:**
    - Design exercises that involve capturing and analysing packets related to common network scenarios.

Conclusion:
Understanding TCP/IP fundamentals, navigating network protocols, and mastering tools like Wireshark are essential skills for any pentester. These skills enable you to uncover vulnerabilities, identify security weaknesses, and strengthen network defences. As you continue your pentesting journey, keep refining your networking knowledge—it's the

foundation upon which you'll build effective penetration testing strategies.

Chapter 4: Information Gathering and Reconnaissance: Laying the Foundation

In the dynamic realm of ethical hacking, a successful penetration test begins with a comprehensive information gathering and reconnaissance phase. This pivotal step lays the groundwork for understanding the target's digital environment, identifying potential vulnerabilities, and formulating effective penetration strategies. This chapter serves as your entry point into the realm of gathering essential intelligence.

The Essence of Passive and Active Reconnaissance: A Dual Approach

1. **Passive Reconnaissance: Observing Stealthily** In the world of ethical hacking, passive reconnaissance stands as a subtle yet vital tactic. It involves the art of gathering information without direct interaction with the target. This method aligns with the principle of minimising exposure and detection, allowing you to extract insights without raising alarms. Passive reconnaissance comprises activities that prioritise discretion:

   - **OSINT (Open-Source Intelligence):** Delve into publicly available information on websites, social media platforms, and online communities. These virtual landscapes often conceal valuable data points that could unveil potential vulnerabilities.
   - **Domain Reconnaissance:** Peel back the layers of a target's online presence by scrutinising domain records, examining DNS

information, and delving into WHOIS databases. These hidden pockets of information offer glimpses into the target's digital identity.

2. **Active Reconnaissance: Probing and Interacting** While passive reconnaissance emphasises subtlety, active reconnaissance takes a bolder approach. This method involves direct interaction with the target, aiming to gather a more comprehensive spectrum of information. Active reconnaissance ventures into a territory of more intrusive actions:

   - **Port Scanning:** Uncover the intricate network landscape by probing and identifying active ports and associated services. This technique provides a window into the architecture of the target's systems.
   - **Ping Sweeping:** Emit a series of network ping requests to gauge the responsiveness of hosts and devices. This manoeuvre unveils live entities within the network infrastructure.

Harnessing Tools: Unveiling the Power of Nmap and Shodan

Nmap (Network Mapper): Unveiling the Network Terrain

In the expansive landscape of ethical hacking, one tool stands out as a beacon of versatility and power: Nmap, the Network Mapper. Imagine Nmap as your virtual compass, guiding you through the intricate paths of network exploration, mapping, and vulnerability assessment. This chapter introduces Nmap, a tool that has earned its place as a trusted companion for ethical hackers seeking to unravel the hidden facets of networks.

A Swiss Army Knife for Network Exploration:

Nmap is akin to a Swiss Army knife—an all-in-one solution designed to serve various purposes within the realm of ethical hacking. It boasts a rich repertoire of functionalities that span beyond mere port scanning. As you navigate its features, you'll discover that Nmap's capabilities include:

- **Port Scanning:** The ability to discover open ports on target systems, providing insight into accessible services.
- **Service Identification:** A skill in identifying the services running behind those open ports, often revealing the software versions in use.
- **Vulnerability Detection:** A knack for highlighting known vulnerabilities that may lurk within the target's services.

Embracing the Power of Nmap:

To harness Nmap's capabilities, you'll step into the world of command-line execution—a realm where text-based commands bring forth remarkable actions. Here's a glimpse of how Nmap's power can be harnessed:

Example Usage: nmap -sV -p 1-1000 <target_IP>

This command unchains Nmap's capabilities to orchestrate a scan across the initial 1000 ports of a specified target IP. But what does this command actually accomplish?

1. **-sV:** This flag indicates that Nmap should perform a service version detection scan. In simpler terms, Nmap will attempt to determine the specific software and its version that is running behind each open port it discovers.
2. **-p 1-1000:** This flag instructs Nmap to scan ports within the range of 1 to 1000. It's a targeted approach that focuses on the commonly used ports where services might be operational.
3. **<target_IP>:** Replace this with the IP address of the target you want to scan. Nmap will direct its attention to this address, examining the ports within the specified range.

The Treasure Hunt Begins:

As Nmap executes the command, it embarks on a digital treasure hunt. It meticulously probes the specified range of ports on the target IP, knocking on the virtual doors of services. Behind each door, Nmap seeks information about the service—details that could include software names and version numbers. This information is invaluable for assessing the potential vulnerabilities associated with these services.

Charting the Uncharted Territories:

In your journey through the world of ethical hacking, Nmap emerges as a trusted companion, helping you chart the uncharted territories of network landscapes. With its port scanning prowess, service identification finesse, and vulnerability detection acumen, Nmap becomes your virtual navigator. As you advance in your ethical hacking pursuits, Nmap's capabilities will grow to be an integral part of your toolkit—a reliable guide that empowers you to uncover network nuances, secure vulnerabilities, and contribute to fortified digital defences.

xercise: Unveiling Network Details with Nmap

In this exercise, you'll put your newfound knowledge of Nmap to the test by conducting a network scan on the previously set up virtual lab. Your objective is to gain insights into the network landscape, identify open ports, and extract service information from a target machine.

Lab Setup:

- Virtual Machine (Target): IP Address - 192.168.0.10
- Virtual Machine (Attacker): IP Address - 192.168.0.20

Instructions:

1. **Open a Terminal:** On your attacker machine, open a terminal window. This is where you'll execute Nmap commands.
2. **Run Nmap Scan:** Execute the following Nmap command to scan the target machine for open ports and service information:

   nmap -sV -p 1-1000 192.168.0.10

2. **Analyse Results:** After the scan completes, observe the output. Nmap will provide you with a list of open ports, the services running on those ports, and their corresponding versions. Pay attention to the information revealed about each service.

3. **Interpret Vulnerabilities:** Use the service information obtained from the scan to research potential vulnerabilities associated with the identified services. Determine whether any of the services are running outdated versions or known vulnerabilities.
4. **Reflect and Plan:** Based on the information gathered, consider the security implications of the open ports and services on the target machine. Reflect on potential attack vectors that could be exploited and devise strategies to enhance the target's security posture.

Exercise Extension (Optional):

- Modify the Nmap command to scan a specific range of ports or target multiple machines in your lab.
- Explore different Nmap scan options (e.g., aggressive scans, script scans) to uncover deeper insights into the target's services and potential vulnerabilities.

Enhancing Network Awareness

This exercise showcases the practical application of Nmap in ethical hacking scenarios. By conducting a network scan, you gained valuable insights into the services running on the target machine and identified potential vulnerabilities. This knowledge equips you with the ability to analyse network landscapes, assess potential risks, and recommend security measures to strengthen the network's defences. As you delve deeper into the world of ethical hacking, Nmap remains a valuable tool in your arsenal for uncovering hidden details within network environments.

Exploring Shodan: Unveiling Publicly Accessible Devices

Shodan, often hailed as "the search engine for the Internet of Things," is a powerful tool that provides an unprecedented glimpse into the digital landscape. It enables ethical hackers, security professionals, and researchers to peer into the world of publicly accessible devices spread across the vast expanse of the internet. By delving into Shodan's capabilities, you open a gateway to uncovering vulnerabilities, misconfigurations, and digital artifacts that might otherwise remain hidden.

Accessing Shodan: A Journey into Digital Discovery

Here's a step-by-step guide on how to access Shodan and perform searches, along with a few examples of search terms:

Step 1: Open Your Web Browser Launch your preferred web browser on your computer or device.

Step 2: Navigate to Shodan's Website Type "https://www.shodan.io/" into your browser's address bar and hit Enter. This will take you to Shodan's official website.

Step 3: Create an Account or Log In If you're new to Shodan, click on the "Sign up" link to create an account. Provide your email address, choose a password, and complete the registration process. If you already have an account, click "Login" and enter your credentials.

Step 4: Access the Shodan Search Bar After logging in, you'll see a search bar at the top of the page. This is where you'll enter your search queries.

Step 5: Enter Your Search Query Type in your desired search query. Here are a few examples of search terms:

- To find open webcams: "webcam"

- To identify unsecured databases: "port:27017"

- To discover exposed RDP services: "port:3389"

- To locate IoT devices: "category:iot"

- To search for Apache HTTP servers: "apache"

- To explore vulnerable Hikvision control panels: "title:'Hikvision'"

Step 6: Press Enter to Perform the Search Hit Enter on your keyboard or click the "Search" button next to the search bar to execute your query.

Step 7: Explore the Search Results Browse through the search results that match your query. Each result provides information about the device, its IP address, open ports, and more.

Step 8: Refine Your Search You can use filters and additional keywords to narrow down your results further. For instance, you can filter results based on location, operating system, or specific services.

Step 9: Explore Devices and Services Click on individual search results to delve deeper into the details of each device or service. Some results may even offer screenshots of web interfaces.

Step 10: Use Results Responsibly Always exercise ethical use of the information you gather from Shodan. Respect the privacy and security of the devices and services you discover, and avoid any unauthorised actions.

By following these steps and using a variety of search terms, you can effectively utilise Shodan to explore publicly accessible devices and services for cybersecurity research and penetration testing purposes.

A Window to the Internet of Things:

Imagine Shodan as a virtual telescope trained on the cosmos of interconnected devices. Just as a telescope unveils celestial bodies, Shodan uncovers the myriad devices that make up the Internet of Things (IoT). These devices range from webcams, routers, and servers to industrial control systems, smart appliances, and even critical infrastructure components. Shodan offers a unique perspective, helping you identify the technology landscape's most visible stars.

Unmatched Exploration:

Shodan's capabilities span far and wide, making it a formidable asset in the ethical hacking arsenal:

- **Device Identification:** Shodan can identify and categorise various devices based on their banners, which are often unique strings of information provided by the devices themselves.

- **Service Enumeration:** It reveals active services running on devices, allowing you to assess potential points of entry.
- **Vulnerability Discovery:** Shodan flags devices with known vulnerabilities, assisting in targeted security assessments.
- **Geographical Insights:** The tool can provide geographic information about devices, helping to understand regional technology trends.

Unlocking a New Dimension of Exploration:

Consider a scenario where you want to assess the security of webcams connected to the internet. Shodan's search capabilities empower you to look for specific criteria:

- **Example Search:** webcam port:80
- This query targets devices with open port 80, commonly used for web services, potentially revealing open webcams.

Similarly, you could search for exposed industrial control systems or routers with vulnerable firmware. The possibilities are vast, and the insights are eye-opening.

A Virtual Compass in the Digital Realm:

Shodan stands as an indispensable tool for those navigating the intricate web of interconnected devices. By peering into publicly accessible devices, you gain insights that shape penetration testing, vulnerability assessments, and security enhancement strategies. As you explore the expansiveness of Shodan's capabilities, remember that responsible use and a commitment to ethical hacking principles are paramount. In your hands, Shodan becomes more than a tool—it transforms into a virtual compass guiding you through the complexities of the digital realm.

Harvesting from Open Sources: A Treasure Trove of Public Data

1. **Google Dorking: Navigating Beyond Standard Searches** Beyond the realm of standard searches lies the realm of Google Dorking. This art involves the adept use of advanced search operators to uncover sensitive data inadvertently exposed online. Google Dorking transcends standard searches:

   Example Search: Envision executing a query such as site:example.com filetype:pdf. This exploration may uncover an assortment of PDF documents nestled within the digital confines of the "example.com" domain.

2. **WHOIS Lookup: Unravelling Domain Identity** WHOIS databases serve as vaults of domain-related information. A WHOIS lookup grants access to registration details encompassing domain ownership, registration dates, and contact particulars.

3. **Social Media and Forums: The Human Touch** In the age of interconnectedness, social media profiles and online forums radiate with insights. Engaging in a process of scrutiny exposes details about the target organisation and individuals affiliated with it.

Here's a list of tools commonly used for information gathering in ethical hacking and pentesting, along with brief explanations of their functionalities, some have already been addressed in this chapter:

theHarvester: A reconnaissance tool that gathers emails, subdomains, hosts, employee names, open ports, and banners from different public sources like search engines, PGP key servers, and Shodan. It helps in building a comprehensive picture of the target's online presence.

Shodan: Often referred to as the "search engine for the Internet of Things," Shodan allows you to explore publicly accessible devices across the internet. It provides details about open ports, services, and potential vulnerabilities in various connected devices.

Censys: Similar to Shodan, Censys focuses on exploring the digital world's exposed devices. It provides detailed information about hosts, protocols, certificates, and services, aiding in vulnerability assessment.

Nmap (Network Mapper): A versatile tool used for network discovery and security auditing. It can scan hosts for open ports, discover services running on those ports, and provide information about the operating systems being used.

Maltego: A visual link analysis tool that helps you identify relationships and connections between entities like domains, IP addresses, and people. It assists in mapping out the target's digital footprint.

Whois: A command-line tool used to retrieve domain registration information. It provides details about the domain owner, registration date, contact information, and more.

DNSDumpster: A tool for gathering information related to DNS records, subdomains, and IP addresses associated with a domain. It assists in mapping out the target's domain infrastructure.

theZoo: A collection of live malware samples and threat intelligence feeds that can be used for analysis and understanding prevalent threats in the wild.

Wayback Machine (Archive.org): A web archive that allows you to view previous versions of websites. It can be useful for historical information gathering and identifying potential vulnerabilities in older versions of websites.

SpiderFoot: An open-source footprinting and reconnaissance tool that automates the process of collecting information about a target. It gathers data from multiple sources, including search engines, social media, domain records, and more.

Google Hacking Database (GHDB): A curated list of Google search queries that can be used to discover sensitive information, vulnerabilities, and exposed data by leveraging Google's indexing capabilities.

Recon-ng: A full-featured reconnaissance framework that provides modules for information gathering from various sources, including social media, search engines, and DNS records.

These tools collectively assist ethical hackers and pentesters in gathering valuable information about the target, aiding them in understanding the target's attack surface and potential vulnerabilities. Keep in mind that responsible and ethical use of these tools is crucial to avoid infringing on privacy and legal boundaries.

Embarking on an Essential Journey

The chapter of information gathering, and reconnaissance serves as the gateway to ethical hacking success. Like intrepid explorers, you navigate the realms of passive and active reconnaissance, each revealing unique facets of the target's digital realm. Armed with the prowess of tools like Nmap and Shodan, you extract valuable intelligence from open sources, transforming information into knowledge. This knowledge fuels your subsequent stages of penetration testing, allowing you to identify vulnerabilities, formulate targeted strategies, and contribute to the fortified security of digital landscapes. As you embark on this essential journey, remember that every bit of information you gather brings you closer to achieving your ethical hacking objectives.

Chapter 5: Scanning and Vulnerability Assessment

Welcome to the exciting realm of scanning and vulnerability assessment. In this chapter, we'll delve into the essential concepts of identifying open ports, uncovering services, conducting vulnerability scans using tools like Nessus, and deciphering scan results. Let's embark on this journey of discovery and fortification!

Identifying Open Ports and Services: Peering into the Network Landscape

1. **Open Ports: Gateways to Services** Think of open ports as virtual gateways through which services communicate. Each open port corresponds to a specific service. For example, port 80 typically hosts HTTP web services, while port 22 is reserved for SSH (Secure Shell).

2. **Service Identification: Revealing Service Details** Services run behind open ports, providing functionality to networked systems. Examples include web servers, email servers, and databases. Service banners reveal crucial information, such as software versions, that help assess potential vulnerabilities.

Conducting Vulnerability Scans with Nessus: Illuminating Weaknesses

1. **Introduction to Nessus: Your Vulnerability Detective** Nessus is a robust vulnerability scanning tool that aids in uncovering security weaknesses within

systems. It detects vulnerabilities, misconfigurations, and potential threats.

2. **Installing and Running Nessus:**
   - o **Step 1:** Download and install Nessus from the official website.
   - o **Step 2:** Launch the Nessus application.
   - o **Step 3:** Access the web interface via your browser (usually at https://localhost:8834).
   - o **Step 4:** Follow the setup wizard to configure Nessus with necessary settings.

3. **Creating a Vulnerability Scan:**
   - o **Step 1:** Define your target by specifying the target IP or range.
   - o **Step 2:** Choose the scan type (e.g., Basic Network Scan, Web Application Scan).
   - o **Step 3:** Configure scan settings, such as port range and scan intensity.

4. **Initiating the Scan:**
   - o **Step 1:** Start the scan and monitor its progress.
   - o **Step 2:** Nessus examines open ports, services, and associated vulnerabilities.

Analysing Scan Results and Prioritising Vulnerabilities: Unlocking Insights

1. **Interpreting Scan Reports:** Nessus generates comprehensive scan reports detailing identified vulnerabilities, affected hosts, and recommended actions. Each vulnerability is categorised by severity.

2. **Understanding Vulnerability Severity Levels:**
   - o **Critical:** Vulnerabilities that pose an immediate and severe threat.

- o **High:** Significant vulnerabilities that require prompt attention.
- o **Medium:** Vulnerabilities that could potentially be exploited.
- o **Low:** Lesser risks that may not warrant immediate action.

3. **Prioritising Remediation Efforts:** Focus on addressing critical and high-severity vulnerabilities first. Work your way down the severity levels, addressing vulnerabilities that align with your organisation's risk tolerance and resources.

CVE (Common Vulnerabilities and Exposures)

This plays a pivotal role in the vulnerability scanning process by offering a standardised framework for identifying and labelling vulnerabilities across various software and hardware systems. Here's how CVEs are utilised during vulnerability scanning, along with guidance on accessing them:

1. **Vulnerability Detection and Identification:** In the vulnerability scanning stage, when a vulnerability scanner detects a potential security flaw within a system, it aims to pinpoint the precise nature of the vulnerability. CVEs come into play as they offer a recognised naming convention and description for each known vulnerability.

2. **CVE Matching:** The scanner cross-references the characteristics of the identified vulnerability with the comprehensive CVE database. If a match is established between the details of the detected vulnerability and an existing CVE entry, the scanner

associates the vulnerability with the corresponding CVE identifier. This correlation provides immediate insight into the vulnerability's nature.

3. **Gathering Contextual Information:** CVE entries go beyond mere identifiers; they supply valuable contextual data. This includes specifics about the vulnerability's severity, affected software versions, potential modes of attack, and recommended steps to mitigate the risk. This information empowers security professionals and administrators to grasp the scope and potential impact of the vulnerability.

4. **Prioritising Response Efforts:** CVEs often carry severity ratings, facilitating the prioritisation of remediation efforts. Vulnerabilities with higher severity ratings or known exploitability are addressed with a heightened sense of urgency. This strategic approach ensures that critical vulnerabilities receive swift attention to mitigate potential breaches.

5. **Guiding Mitigation and Resolution:** CVE information serves as a roadmap for devising effective strategies to mitigate or remediate the vulnerability. This might entail applying available patches, adjusting configurations, or implementing temporary workarounds to minimise the vulnerability's impact.

6. **Incorporating in Reports and Communication:** Vulnerability scanning reports typically feature the CVE identifiers associated with detected vulnerabilities. This inclusion streamlines communication by enabling security practitioners to succinctly communicate the nature and implications of the vulnerabilities to relevant stakeholders.

7. **Accessing CVE Information:** To access the wealth of CVE information, you can use the official CVE database, available at https://cve.mitre.org. This resource allows you to search for specific CVE identifiers, explore vulnerability details, and gather the necessary context for addressing security issues.

8. **Ongoing Vigilance:** CVEs are dynamic, continually evolving with additional data such as references to advisories, patches, and other relevant materials. A proactive vulnerability management strategy involves consistent monitoring of CVE databases to stay informed about new vulnerabilities and recommended mitigation actions.

In essence, CVEs act as a lingua franca for discussing vulnerabilities during the vulnerability scanning stage. Their standardisation enhances communication, enables accurate vulnerability identification, and streamlines effective mitigation efforts across diverse technological landscapes.

There are several other options for conducting vulnerability scanning apart from Nessus. Here are a few alternatives that you can explore:

1. **Nexpose by Rapid7:** Nexpose is a vulnerability management solution that offers vulnerability scanning and assessment capabilities. It provides a detailed view of the vulnerabilities present in your network, prioritises them based on risk, and offers suggestions for remediation. Nexpose is known for its intuitive interface and ease of use.

2. **Qualys Vulnerability Management:** Qualys offers a cloud-based vulnerability management platform that includes vulnerability scanning, assessment, and reporting. It can scan both on-premises and cloud environments, providing real-time insights into vulnerabilities across your infrastructure.

3. **Acunetix:** Acunetix is a specialised vulnerability scanner that focuses on web application security. It scans web applications for vulnerabilities such as SQL injection, cross-site scripting (XSS), and more. Acunetix helps identify and mitigate security flaws in your web applications.

4. **Burp Suite:** While primarily known as a web security testing tool, Burp Suite also includes vulnerability scanning capabilities. It can identify security issues in web applications, including potential vulnerabilities related to input validation, authentication, and session management.

5. **Retina by BeyondTrust:** Retina is a vulnerability management solution that offers both agent-based and agentless scanning options. It provides insights into vulnerabilities across a wide range of assets, including servers, workstations, and network devices.

6. **Open Source Vulnerability Database (OSVDB):** OSVDB is a community-driven vulnerability database that provides vulnerability information, including descriptions, impact assessments, and references. While not a scanning tool itself, it can be used to research and identify vulnerabilities.

When selecting a vulnerability scanning tool, consider factors such as your organisation's requirements, the types of assets you need to scan, ease of use, reporting capabilities, and whether the tool supports both internal and external network scanning. Each tool has its strengths and may be better suited for specific use cases, so it's recommended to evaluate a few options to find the one that aligns with your needs.

Illuminating Vulnerabilities, Bolstering Security

As you journey through the realms of scanning and vulnerability assessment, remember that each scan unveils a unique layer of your network's security landscape. Identifying open ports, understanding services, and conducting vulnerability scans empower you to take proactive measures to enhance your digital defences. Nessus, your trusty vulnerability detective, provides invaluable insights into potential weaknesses. Analysing scan results with a discerning eye and prioritising vulnerabilities bring you closer to building a resilient and fortified digital environment. With your newfound skills, you're equipped to identify and address vulnerabilities that could compromise the integrity and security of your systems.

Hands-On Exercise: Uncover Vulnerabilities with Nessus

In this hands-on exercise, you will step into the shoes of an ethical hacker and conduct a vulnerability assessment using Nessus on your previously set up virtual lab. Through this exercise, you will gain practical experience in running a vulnerability scan, interpreting the scan results, and prioritising vulnerabilities for remediation.

Lab Setup:

- Virtual Machine (Target): IP Address - 192.168.0.10
- Virtual Machine (Attacker): IP Address - 192.168.0.20
- Nessus Installed and Configured on Attacker Machine

Instructions:

1. **Open Nessus Web Interface:** Launch a web browser on your attacker machine and access the Nessus web interface. This is usually done by navigating to https://localhost:8834 or the URL provided during Nessus installation.
2. **Log In and Set Up a Scan:**
   - Log in to the Nessus web interface using your credentials.
   - Create a new scan by clicking on the "Scans" tab and then selecting "New Scan."
   - Configure the scan settings:
     - **Name:** Give your scan a descriptive name.
     - **Targets:** Enter the IP address of your target virtual machine (192.168.0.10).
     - **Scan Type:** Choose a scan type based on your goals (e.g., Basic Network Scan).
     - **Scan Settings:** Configure options such as port range and scan intensity.
3. **Initiate the Scan:**
   - Click "Save" to create the scan.

- Start the scan by clicking on the scan name and then clicking "Launch."

4. **Monitor Scan Progress:** Observe the scan progress as Nessus examines the target machine for vulnerabilities. This process may take some time, depending on the complexity of the scan and the network.

5. **Review Scan Results:** Once the scan is complete, access the scan report to review the identified vulnerabilities. Pay attention to the severity levels assigned to each vulnerability.

6. **Prioritise Vulnerabilities:**

   - Focus on vulnerabilities marked as "Critical" and "High" severity. These are the most urgent ones to address.
   - Analyse the description and solution details provided for each vulnerability to understand its impact and recommended remediation steps.

7. **Plan Remediation:** Based on the vulnerabilities identified, create a plan for addressing them. Consider factors such as the potential impact of vulnerabilities on your network and the availability of patches or fixes.

Exercise Extension (Optional):

- Run additional scans with different settings, such as increasing the port range or adjusting the scan intensity.

- Explore Nessus's advanced options, such as configuring credentials to perform authenticated scans for deeper insights.
- Research and experiment with interpreting vulnerability details and generating more customised reports.

Conclusion: Strengthening Network Security

Through this exercise, you've gained hands-on experience in using Nessus to conduct a vulnerability assessment. By interpreting scan results and prioritising vulnerabilities, you've taken a crucial step towards enhancing your network's security posture. As you progress in your ethical hacking journey, remember that vulnerability assessment is an ongoing process, and continuous scanning and remediation efforts are essential to safeguarding your digital environment against potential threats.

Hands-On Exercise: Uncover Vulnerabilities with OpenVAS

In this hands-on exercise, you'll step into the world of vulnerability assessment using OpenVAS (Open Vulnerability Assessment System). You'll explore the process of setting up and running a vulnerability scan, interpreting scan results, and prioritising vulnerabilities for remediation.

Lab Setup:

- Virtual Machine (Target): IP Address - 192.168.0.10
- Virtual Machine (Attacker): IP Address - 192.168.0.20
- OpenVAS Installed and Configured on Attacker Machine

Instructions:

1. **Access OpenVAS Web Interface:** Launch a web browser on your attacker machine and access the OpenVAS web interface. This is usually done by navigating to https://localhost:9392 or the URL provided during OpenVAS installation.
2. **Log In and Set Up a Scan:**
    - Log in using your OpenVAS credentials.
    - Create a new target by clicking on "Configuration" and then selecting "Targets."
    - Add a new target by specifying the IP address of your target virtual machine (192.168.0.10).
3. **Create a New Task for Vulnerability Scan:**
    - Navigate to "Scans" and click on "Task Wizard."
    - Select the target you created in the previous step.
    - Choose the "Full and fast ultimate" scan configuration (or another appropriate option).
4. **Initiate the Scan:**
    - Click "Create" to set up the task.
    - Start the task by clicking on the task name and then selecting "Start."
5. **Monitor Scan Progress:** Observe the scan progress as OpenVAS scans the target machine for

vulnerabilities. Depending on the scan configuration and network size, this process may take some time.

6. **Review Scan Results**: Once the scan completes, access the scan report to review the identified vulnerabilities. OpenVAS categorises vulnerabilities by severity.

7. **Prioritise Vulnerabilities:**
    o Focus on vulnerabilities marked as "High" and "Medium" severity. These require prompt attention.
    o Examine the details and recommended solutions for each vulnerability to understand their impact and possible mitigation steps.

8. **Plan Remediation:** Based on the vulnerabilities identified, create a plan for addressing them. Consider factors such as the potential risk and the availability of patches or fixes.

Exercise Extension (Optional):

- Run additional scans with different configurations to explore OpenVAS's flexibility.
- Experiment with scheduling recurring scans to automate the vulnerability assessment process.
- Research and experiment with interpreting vulnerability details and generating customised reports.

Conclusion: Empowering Network Security

Through this exercise, you've gained hands-on experience in using OpenVAS for vulnerability assessment. You've witnessed the process of initiating scans, interpreting results, and prioritising vulnerabilities for remediation. As you advance in your ethical hacking journey, remember that vulnerability assessment is an ongoing effort. Regular scans and timely remediation are crucial in maintaining a secure network environment and protecting your systems from potential threats.

Chapter 6: Exploitation Techniques - Unveiling the Art of Ethical Hacking

Exploitation in the Context of Ethical Hacking

Exploitation, in the realm of ethical hacking and cybersecurity, refers to the practice of taking advantage of vulnerabilities, weaknesses, or security flaws in software, systems, or networks with the goal of gaining unauthorised access, control, or privileges. Ethical hackers use exploitation techniques to demonstrate the potential risks and impact of these vulnerabilities, assisting organisations in identifying and addressing security weaknesses before malicious hackers can exploit them.

In other words, exploitation involves demonstrating the real-world consequences of vulnerabilities by simulating an attack scenario. This is done in a controlled and authorised manner, with the primary objective of helping organisations understand the urgency of patching vulnerabilities and implementing security measures.

Key points to understand about exploitation:

1. **Authorised Activity:** Ethical hackers receive permission from the organisation's owners to conduct exploitation activities. This ensures that the actions taken are legal and within the scope of ethical hacking.
2. **Purposeful Demonstration:** Exploitation is not intended to cause harm but to showcase how a malicious attacker could potentially compromise a system or gain unauthorised access.

3. **Proof of Concept:** Ethical hackers often develop proofs of concept (PoCs) that illustrate how a vulnerability can be exploited. These PoCs help organisations visualise the threat and understand the necessary actions to mitigate it.
4. **Variety of Techniques:** Exploitation techniques can include buffer overflow attacks, SQL injection, cross-site scripting (XSS), remote code execution (RCE), privilege escalation, and more.
5. **Responsibility and Reporting:** Ethical hackers are responsible for reporting their findings to the organisation's stakeholders, including detailed information about the vulnerabilities and the steps taken to exploit them. This information assists in the remediation process.
6. **Knowledge Transfer:** Through exploitation, organisations gain insights into potential risks and can make informed decisions about prioritising and addressing vulnerabilities.
7. **Learning and Defence:** Ethical hackers learn from successful exploitation scenarios, allowing them to design better defence mechanisms and security strategies to prevent such attacks.

Exploitation serves as a critical component of ethical hacking by shedding light on the real-world impact of vulnerabilities. By conducting controlled and authorised exploitation activities, ethical hackers contribute to the overall improvement of cybersecurity practices and help organisations fortify their digital defences against potential threats.

Exploring Common Exploitation Methods: The Path to Control

Understanding Exploitation: The Bridge to Control
Exploitation refers to the practice of leveraging vulnerabilities in software or systems to gain unauthorised access, control, or privileges. Ethical hackers utilise this knowledge to identify weaknesses and assist in fortifying digital defences.

Common Exploitation Techniques:

- **Buffer Overflow:** Overflowing a program's buffer to manipulate memory and execute malicious code.
- **SQL Injection:** Injecting malicious SQL queries to manipulate databases and retrieve unauthorised information.
- **Cross-Site Scripting (XSS):** Injecting malicious scripts into web applications to steal user data or compromise systems.
- **Remote Code Execution (RCE):** Exploiting vulnerabilities to execute arbitrary code on a remote system.
- **Privilege Escalation:** Elevating user privileges to gain unauthorised access to sensitive resources.

Metasploit: The Swiss Army Knife of Penetration Testing

Metasploit is an immensely powerful and widely-used penetration testing framework designed to assist security professionals, ethical hackers, and penetration testers in identifying and exploiting vulnerabilities in software systems, networks, and applications. Developed by Rapid7, Metasploit simplifies the process of discovering security weaknesses and demonstrating the potential impact of those vulnerabilities.

Key aspects of Metasploit:

1. **Comprehensive Toolset:** Metasploit provides a vast array of tools, exploits, payloads, auxiliary modules, and post-exploitation modules. It covers every phase of a penetration test, from reconnaissance to exploitation, post-exploitation, and reporting.

2. **Exploit Development:** One of Metasploit's highlights is its ability to automate the development and execution of exploits. It offers a repository of pre-built exploits that can be easily customised and adapted to specific vulnerabilities.

3. **Payloads:** A payload is the code executed on a compromised system after a successful exploit. Metasploit offers a variety of payloads designed for different purposes, such as gaining remote access, extracting data, or launching further attacks.

4. **Exploitation Techniques:** Metasploit encompasses a range of exploitation techniques, including remote code execution, buffer overflow, and more. These techniques help ethical hackers demonstrate the potential impact of vulnerabilities.

5. **Post-Exploitation Modules:** After a successful exploit, Metasploit provides post-exploitation modules that allow ethical hackers to gather information, elevate privileges, pivot to other systems, and establish persistence.

6. **Community and Collaboration:** Metasploit has a vibrant and active user community that contributes to its continuous development. Users share exploits, modules, and research findings, enhancing the framework's capabilities.

7. **Integration:** Metasploit can be integrated with other tools and frameworks, making it a versatile choice for penetration testers and security professionals.

8. **Ease of Use:** Despite its advanced capabilities, Metasploit is designed to be user-friendly. It offers both command-line and graphical interfaces, catering to users with varying levels of expertise.

9. **Ethical Use:** Metasploit is an essential tool for ethical hackers and security practitioners who have received proper authorisation to conduct penetration testing. Its purpose is to help organisations identify vulnerabilities and strengthen their security measures.

In summary, Metasploit is a vital tool for ethical hackers and penetration testers, providing them with the means to simulate real-world attack scenarios in a controlled environment. By leveraging its exploit development, payload delivery, and post-exploitation features, professionals can uncover vulnerabilities and assist organisations in fortifying their digital defences against potential threats.

1. **Installation and Setup:**
   o **Step 1:** Install Metasploit on your system. For example, on Kali Linux, use apt-get install metasploit-framework.

- Step 2: Launch Metasploit by entering msfconsole in the terminal.
2. **Basic Metasploit Commands:**
    - **search <keyword>:** Search for exploits or payloads using keywords.
    - **use <module>:** Select a specific module for exploitation.
    - **show options:** Display the configurable options for the selected module.
    - **set <option> <value>:** Set the values for module options.
    - **exploit:** Execute the selected exploit.

Crafting and Launching Attacks Against Vulnerabilities: Hands-On Exploration

1. **Selecting a Vulnerability and Exploit:**
    - Identify a target system and the associated vulnerability (e.g., a known CVE).
    - Search Metasploit for an exploit module that targets the identified vulnerability.
2. **Configuring the Exploit:**
    - Use the use command to select the desired exploit module.
    - View and set the required options using the show options and set commands.
3. **Launching the Attack:**
    - Once all required options are configured, execute the exploit using the exploit command.
4. **Understanding Post-Exploitation:**
    - Successful exploitation may grant you access to the target system.

- Explore post-exploitation modules in Metasploit to gather information, elevate privileges, and establish persistence.

Ethical Responsibility: The Heart of Exploitation Techniques

1. **Ethics and Legality:**
   - Ethical hackers must use their skills responsibly and within the boundaries of the law.
   - Obtain explicit permission before conducting any penetration testing or exploitation activities.
2. **Responsible Reporting:**
   - If vulnerabilities are discovered, report them to the appropriate parties for remediation.
   - Avoid causing harm or unauthorised disruption to systems.

Here are some examples of other exploitation tools commonly used by ethical hackers and penetration testers:

1. **Canvas:** Canvas is a commercial exploitation framework developed by Immunity Inc. It offers a range of exploits and payloads for testing various vulnerabilities in systems and applications. Canvas is known for its user-friendly interface and extensive exploit database.

2. **Core Impact:** Core Impact is a commercial penetration testing tool that includes an extensive set of exploits, payloads, and post-exploitation modules. It focuses on simulating real-world attack

scenarios and provides a comprehensive reporting system.

3. **BeEF (Browser Exploitation Framework):** BeEF is an open-source tool designed for exploiting web browsers and their vulnerabilities. It helps ethical hackers assess client-side vulnerabilities, conduct browser-based attacks, and gather information from compromised systems.

4. **SET (Social-Engineer Toolkit):** The Social-Engineer Toolkit is an open-source framework that focuses on social engineering attacks. It includes a variety of attack vectors, such as spear phishing, credential harvesting, and malicious USB attacks.

5. **Empire:** Empire is an open-source post-exploitation framework that offers a collection of modules for maintaining control over compromised systems. It supports a range of communication methods and provides features for lateral movement and persistence.

6. **CrackMapExec (CME):** CrackMapExec is an open-source post-exploitation tool that focuses on credential theft, lateral movement, and privilege escalation in Windows environments. It can assist in mapping the network, identifying vulnerable systems, and executing commands on compromised hosts.

7. **Mimikatz:** Mimikatz is a popular open-source tool used for extracting credentials from Windows systems. It can retrieve passwords, hashes, and other authentication data stored in memory, making it valuable for privilege escalation.

8. **PowerShell Empire:** PowerShell Empire is an open-source post-exploitation framework that leverages PowerShell to maintain control over compromised systems. It provides a variety of modules for tasks such as privilege escalation, data exfiltration, and lateral movement.

9. **Bettercap:** Bettercap is an open-source network monitoring and attack tool that focuses on network-level attacks, man-in-the-middle attacks, and session hijacking. It provides a range of capabilities for intercepting and manipulating network traffic.

10. **Armitage:** Armitage is a graphical front-end for the Metasploit framework. It simplifies the process of using Metasploit by providing an intuitive interface for selecting exploits, managing sessions, and conducting post-exploitation activities.

These tools, like Metasploit, are designed to be used responsibly and ethically within authorised penetration testing scenarios. Each tool specialises in different aspects of exploitation, post-exploitation, or social engineering attacks, catering to the diverse needs of ethical hackers and security professionals.

Conclusion: Empowering Defence through Offense

As you conclude this exploration of exploitation techniques, remember that the knowledge gained equips you to think like a hacker and devise strategies to strengthen your systems' security. Detailed descriptions of each tool could warrant a book on their own, therefore this chapter is designed as a guide to start you on your journey.

We examined Metasploit in more detail that provides a controlled environment to hone your skills and test defences against potential threats. The key lies in ethical responsibility—to use your expertise to safeguard digital landscapes rather than undermine them. With the power of knowledge and ethical principles, you pave the way for a more secure and resilient digital world.

Chapter 7: Post-Exploitation and Lateral Movement - Navigating Beyond the Breach

n the dynamic realm of cybersecurity, breaching a system serves as the initial key to an intricate puzzle. Yet, it's crucial to understand that breaching merely opens the door—it's what lies beyond that truly matters. This pivotal chapter unravels the compelling narrative that follows a successful hack: the realm of Post-Exploitation and Lateral Movement. Here, we journey through uncharted territories, peering beyond the breach to comprehend the ramifications of our actions.

Post-Exploitation: Unveiling the Pathways to Control

Once a breach is accomplished, the landscape shifts from penetration to persistence. Post-exploitation techniques come into play as we explore the art of establishing and maintaining access within compromised systems. It's not just about entry; it's about forging a lasting presence. Here, the ethical hacker must master the delicate balance of remaining concealed while ensuring ongoing control.

Privilege Escalation: Elevating Authority Responsibly

Within the realm of privilege escalation, the journey involves ascending the ladder of system authority. The ethical hacker learns to navigate the intricate pathways of both vertical and horizontal privilege escalation. It's the art of ethically climbing higher by exploiting misconfigurations and vulnerabilities, all the while conscious of the implications of wielding elevated privileges.

Privilege Escalation: Gaining Higher Authority

Privilege escalation is a critical phase in post-exploitation, where an ethical hacker aims to elevate their level of access within a compromised system. This phase demonstrates the potential consequences of a successful breach by showcasing how an attacker could gain higher authority and control over the system.

Understanding Privilege Levels:

Most operating systems employ a hierarchical privilege structure, with different user accounts having varying levels of authority. Privilege escalation exploits vulnerabilities or misconfigurations to move from a lower privilege level to a higher one. For example, moving from a standard user to an administrator or root level.

Common Privilege Escalation Techniques:

1. **Kernel Exploits:** Exploiting vulnerabilities in the operating system's kernel to gain elevated privileges.
2. **Misconfigured Services:** Taking advantage of services or applications with improper configurations that allow unauthorised privilege escalation.
3. **Weak File Permissions:** Exploiting poorly set file and directory permissions to gain unauthorised access to sensitive files.
4. **Credentials in Memory:** Exploiting situations where plaintext or hashed credentials are stored in memory, allowing an attacker to retrieve and use them.

Hands-On Lab: Privilege Escalation

Scenario: You have successfully exploited a vulnerable application on a Linux system and gained access as a low-privileged user. Your goal is to escalate privileges to the root level.

Steps:

1. **Enumerate the System:** Use tools like "ps" to identify running processes and "id" to identify your current user's privileges.
2. **Search for Vulnerabilities:** Search for known vulnerabilities using tools like "searchsploit" to identify potential privilege escalation vulnerabilities related to the system or applications.
3. **Check Misconfigured Services:** Use tools like "netstat" or "ss" to identify open ports and running services. Research if any of these services have known vulnerabilities or misconfigurations that can be exploited.
4. **Weak File Permissions:** Check for files with weak permissions that might contain sensitive information. Common locations include configuration files and system scripts.
5. **Kernel Exploits:** If you have kernel-level access, search for kernel exploits that match the system's version and architecture. Compile and run the exploit if applicable.

Ethical Considerations: Always perform these activities in a controlled environment with proper authorisation. Privilege escalation should only be conducted to demonstrate vulnerabilities and educate on potential threats.

Tools:

- LinEnum or Linux Exploit Suggester for system enumeration
- Searchsploit for searching known vulnerabilities
- GTFOBins for privilege escalation techniques using common binaries
- ExploitDB for kernel exploits

Consequences and Takeaways: Privilege escalation showcases the gravity of successful exploitation. By demonstrating how attackers can gain higher authority, ethical hackers emphasise the importance of robust security measures, including proper system configurations, access controls, and continuous vulnerability assessments. This phase underscores the need for organisations to implement strong defence mechanisms against potential breaches.

Lateral Movement: Navigating Networks Strategically

Lateral movement takes us on a journey through interconnected systems and networks. It's the essence of controlled exploration—navigating the terrain with precision and purpose. Here, we uncover methods to traverse networks, understand relationships between systems, and strategically identify new targets. Yet, this movement is not about causing chaos; it's about revealing vulnerabilities with the intention of fortifying defences.

The Consequences of Mastery: Ethical Responsibility

As we embark on this journey of post-exploitation and lateral movement, it's imperative to carry the weight of ethical responsibility. Every action taken within these realms must align with ethical guidelines and lawful boundaries. Each advancement within the system comes with potential consequences, underscoring the importance of wielding knowledge with prudence and care.

In the end, this chapter is a testament to the fact that ethical hacking transcends mere technical prowess. It's a journey that bridges the realms of offense and defence, strategy and responsibility. As we delve into the exploration of post-exploitation and lateral movement, we not only uncover vulnerabilities but also uncover our role as stewards of digital security—guardians dedicated to strengthening the digital landscape.

Privilege Escalation Lab: Gaining Root Access

Objective: In this lab, you will simulate a scenario where you have gained initial access to a Linux system as a low-privileged user. Your goal is to escalate your privileges to gain root access, demonstrating the potential consequences of a privilege escalation vulnerability.

Requirements:

- Virtualisation software (e.g., VirtualBox)
- Kali Linux virtual machine (attacker)

- Vulnerable Linux virtual machine (target)

Setup:

1. **Prepare the Target VM:**

   - Download a vulnerable VM image (e.g., Metasploitable2 or VulnHub VMs).
   - Import the VM into your virtualisation software.
   - Start the VM and take note of its IP address (e.g., 192.168.1.100).

2. **Prepare the Attacker VM (Kali Linux):**

   - Download and set up Kali Linux in your virtualisation software.
   - Ensure the Kali VM and the target VM are on the same network.

Lab Steps:

1. **Initial Access:**

   - Use the available exploit to gain access to the target system as a low-privileged user (e.g., SSH credentials, web application vulnerability).

2. **Enumeration:**

   - Run basic enumeration commands (e.g., id, whoami, ls, ps) to gather information about your current user and the system.

3. **Vulnerability Research:**

   - Search for known privilege escalation vulnerabilities associated with the target's operating system and applications using "searchsploit" or other vulnerability databases.

4. **Misconfigured Services:**

   - Identify open ports and running services on the target system using tools like "netstat" or "ss."
   - Research if any services have known vulnerabilities or misconfigurations that could lead to privilege escalation.

5. **Weak File Permissions:**

   - Search for files with weak permissions that may contain sensitive information. Check common locations such as configuration files.
   - Attempt to read or modify these files to demonstrate potential consequences.

6. **Kernel Exploits:**

   - If you have the necessary access, search for kernel exploits that match the target system's version and architecture.
   - Compile and run the exploit if applicable, demonstrating the potential for privilege escalation through kernel vulnerabilities.

Ethical Considerations: Perform this lab in a controlled environment with proper authorisation. Ensure you have the right to test the target system for vulnerabilities and escalate privileges. Do not use these techniques on systems you don't own or have explicit permission to test.

Takeaways: This lab emphasises the importance of securing systems against privilege escalation vulnerabilities. It also underscores the need for regular vulnerability assessments and proper system configurations to prevent unauthorised users from gaining elevated privileges. By simulating privilege escalation, you can educate yourself and others on potential risks and motivate proactive security measures.

Chapter 8: Web Application Security Testing - Safeguarding the Digital Front Door

In the interconnected world of cyberspace, web applications serve as the digital front doors to organisations, holding a wealth of information and functionality. However, with great power comes great responsibility. This chapter embarks on the journey of Web Application Security Testing—a critical discipline that seeks to fortify these digital portals against vulnerabilities and potential breaches.

Introduction to OWASP Top Ten Vulnerabilities: Before delving into testing methodologies, it's crucial to understand the landscape of common web application vulnerabilities. The Open Web Application Security Project (OWASP) Top Ten is a list of the most critical security risks facing web applications. These vulnerabilities, if left unaddressed, can expose sensitive data and compromise system integrity. We explore each vulnerability, from injection attacks to broken authentication, providing insights into their implications and consequences.

Using Tools Like Burp Suite for Web App Testing: Burp Suite emerges as a stalwart companion in the journey of web application testing. This toolset empowers ethical hackers with features for mapping, scanning, and identifying vulnerabilities in web applications. We dive into hands-on tutorials, guiding you through the process of intercepting and modifying requests, performing active and passive scans, and leveraging extensions to enhance testing capabilities.

Writing Secure Code and Understanding Common Vulnerabilities: As the old adage goes, "Prevention is better than cure." Understanding the anatomy of common vulnerabilities enables developers to write secure code from the ground up. We explore the likes of SQL injection, Cross-Site Scripting (XSS), Cross-Site Request Forgery (CSRF), and more. Through real-world examples, we shed light on how these vulnerabilities can be exploited and impart strategies to mitigate them during the development phase.

Hands-On Lab: Testing for Common Vulnerabilities with Burp Suite

Scenario: You're tasked with testing a web application for common vulnerabilities using Burp Suite.

Steps:

1. **Set Up Burp Suite:**

   - Download and install Burp Suite.
   - Configure your browser to use Burp Suite as a proxy.

2. **Discovering and Mapping the Application:**

   - Use Burp Suite's Spider tool to map out the application's structure and identify all accessible endpoints.

3. **Intercept and Modify Requests:**

   - Intercept requests using Burp Proxy to analyse and manipulate them before they reach the server.

- Modify parameters and observe how the application responds.

4. **Active Scanning:**

   - Use Burp Scanner to perform active scans for common vulnerabilities like XSS, SQL injection, and more.
   - Review scan results and understand the vulnerabilities' impact.

5. **Manual Testing:**

   - Explore different input fields for potential injection vulnerabilities.
   - Test for XSS by injecting malicious scripts and observing the application's behaviour.

6. **Understanding the Vulnerabilities:**

   - Review the impact of successful attacks, discussing potential consequences and data exposure.

Ethical Responsibility and Secure Development: Web application security testing is not just about finding vulnerabilities—it's about cultivating a security mindset. Developers and testers alike bear the responsibility of ensuring that applications are robust against threats. This chapter underscores the collaborative effort needed to create a secure digital landscape.

As you journey through the realm of web application security testing, you emerge armed with the ability to assess and enhance the security posture of digital front doors. By understanding vulnerabilities, using sophisticated tools, and championing secure coding practices, you contribute to a safer digital world—one application at a time.

Hands-On Lab: Web Application Security Testing with OWASP and Burp Suite

Objective: In this lab, you will explore the fundamentals of web application security testing using the OWASP Top Ten vulnerabilities as a guide. You will use Burp Suite, a powerful testing tool, to discover, analyse, and mitigate common web application vulnerabilities.

Lab Setup:

- Attacker VM: Kali Linux with Burp Suite installed.
- Target VM: Vulnerable web application (e.g., DVWA or Mutillidae).

Steps:

1. **Mapping the Application:**

   - Launch Burp Suite and set up your browser to use Burp as a proxy.
   - Navigate to the target application in your browser.
   - Use Burp's Spider tool to crawl the application, mapping out its structure and identifying accessible endpoints.

2. **Intercepting Requests:**

- In Burp Suite, navigate to the Proxy tab and enable Intercept.
- Browse the application and observe the intercepted requests and responses.

Modify request parameters using Burp's Intercept feature and observe changes in application behaviour. Modifying request parameters using Burp Suite's Intercept feature allows you to manipulate the data being sent to the web application and observe how it affects the application's behaviour. Here's a step-by-step guide on how to do this:

1. Intercepting Requests with Burp Suite:

- Open Burp Suite and ensure it's configured as a proxy for your web browser. Set your browser to use Burp as a proxy (typically, you set the proxy settings in your browser's network settings).

- In Burp Suite, go to the "Proxy" tab.

- Ensure that the "Intercept is on" button is active (it should be red). This means Burp is intercepting requests and responses between your browser and the web server.

2. Navigating to the Target Web Application:

- In your web browser, navigate to the target web application or webpage you want to test.

3. Modifying Request Parameters:

- As you interact with the web application (e.g., filling out forms, submitting data), Burp Suite will capture the HTTP requests being made.
- When you want to modify a request parameter, Burp Suite will intercept it before it reaches the server. You'll see the request in the Intercept tab.
- Locate the request in the Intercept tab and click on it to open it.

- Within the request, you'll find parameters that you can modify. For example, if you're testing a search function, you might have a parameter like ?q=search-term. You can modify search-term to something else to test for vulnerabilities.

- Make the desired changes to the parameter value. For instance, you can change the search term to ' to test for SQL injection or insert <script>alert('XSS')</script> to test for Cross-Site Scripting (XSS).

4. Forwarding the Modified Request:

- After making the changes, click the "Forward" button in Burp Suite to send the modified request to the server.

5. Observing Application Behaviour:

- Observe how the web application responds to the modified request. Pay attention to any changes in behaviour, such as error messages, unexpected output, or unusual responses.

6. Analysing the Results:

- Based on the application's response, you can assess whether the modification resulted in any security vulnerabilities. For example, if you receive an error message that indicates a SQL error, it may suggest a SQL injection vulnerability.

By using Burp Suite's Intercept feature in this manner, you can actively test and manipulate request parameters to identify and understand potential security issues within a web application.

3. **Active Scanning for Vulnerabilities:**

- Use Burp Scanner to perform active scans on the target application.
- Focus on vulnerabilities from the OWASP Top Ten list: XSS, SQL injection, CSRF, etc.
- Review scan results, understand the vulnerabilities detected, and explore the impact.

4. **Manual Testing for XSS:**

- Identify input fields that may be vulnerable to Cross-Site Scripting (XSS) attacks.
- Inject a simple script (e.g., <script>alert('XSS')</script>) into the input field.

- Observe if the script executes and triggers an alert.

5. **SQL Injection Testing:**

Step 1: Locate Input Fields: Identify an input field in the web application where SQL injection might be possible. This is typically a field that interacts with a database, such as a search or login field.

Step 2: Attempt Basic SQL Injection: Inject a single quote (') or double dash (--) to the input parameter to see if the application is vulnerable to SQL injection.

Step 3: Observe Application's Response: Observe how the application responds to the injected input. If you see error messages, unusual behaviour, or data being displayed that shouldn't be, it's an indication of a potential SQL injection vulnerability.

Example Commands:

Assuming you're testing a search input field on a website:

1. **Locate Input Fields:** Identify the search input field on the website where you suspect SQL injection might be possible.

2. **Attempt Basic SQL Injection:** Try injecting a single quote (') to the input field:

   ' or 1=1 --

2. **Observe Application's Response:**

- If the application responds normally and displays results as expected, it may not be vulnerable.
- If you see an error message like "Database error" or if the application behaves unexpectedly, it could be a sign of vulnerability.

Remember, this is a simple example, and real-world SQL injection attacks can be more complex. Additionally, ethical considerations are important—perform these tests only on systems for which you have explicit permission

6. **Understanding and Mitigating Vulnerabilities:**

- For each vulnerability detected, discuss the potential consequences and risks.
- Explore how to mitigate these vulnerabilities during the development phase.

Ethical Considerations: Perform this lab in a controlled environment with proper authorisation. Only test applications you have permission to test. Do not attempt these techniques on live, production systems.

Takeaways: This hands-on lab empowers you to immerse yourself in the world of web application security testing. By using Burp Suite and OWASP's Top Ten vulnerabilities, you gain practical experience in identifying and understanding common vulnerabilities that could compromise the security of web applications. Armed with knowledge and tools, you contribute to the creation of a more secure digital landscape.

Want to explore further?

The OWASP (Open Web Application Security Project) provides extensive documentation and tutorials to help you understand and address web application security issues. Here's how you can access their resources:

1. **OWASP Top Ten:** The OWASP Top Ten is a well-known list of the most critical web application security risks. You can find detailed explanations and examples for each vulnerability on the OWASP Top Ten page.

2. **OWASP Web Security Testing Guide:** This guide provides in-depth tutorials and methodologies for web application security testing. It covers various testing techniques, including those related to the OWASP Top Ten vulnerabilities.

3. **OWASP Juice Shop:** Juice Shop is a purposely vulnerable web application that you can use to practice your web application security testing skills. It's a hands-on way to learn about real-world vulnerabilities.

4. **OWASP WebGoat:** WebGoat is another educational project that allows you to learn about various web application vulnerabilities and how to exploit or defend against them. It provides practical examples and exercises.

5. **OWASP YouTube Channel:** OWASP maintains a YouTube channel with video tutorials, presentations, and talks related to web application security. You can find a wide range of content from experts in the field. Visit the OWASP YouTube channel

6. **OWASP Cheat Sheets:** OWASP provides cheat sheets that offer concise, practical guides for developers and testers on secure coding practices and addressing various vulnerabilities.

7. **OWASP Community:** Engage with the OWASP community through forums, mailing lists, and local chapters to connect with experts, ask questions, and share experiences.

By exploring these OWASP resources, you'll have access to a wealth of knowledge, tutorials, and tools that can help you enhance your understanding of web application security and strengthen your skills in testing and mitigating vulnerabilities.

Chapter 9: Wireless Network Pentesting - Unravelling the Invisible Threads

In the realm of digital connectivity, wireless networks weave a tapestry of convenience, but they also expose vulnerabilities that can be exploited. This chapter delves into the intricacies of Wireless Network Pentesting—a discipline that empowers you to scrutinise, understand, and fortify wireless environments against potential breaches.

Cracking WEP/WPA/WPA2 Passwords: Wireless networks are often protected by passwords. In this section, we'll explore how to crack WEP, WPA, and WPA2 passwords using tools like Aircrack-ng. We'll learn the differences between encryption methods and walk through step-by-step instructions to launch dictionary attacks and capture handshakes for further analysis.

Let's delve deeper into the details of each wireless encryption protocol: WEP, WPA, WPA2, and WPA3.

In the world of wireless networks, encryption protocols play a pivotal role in safeguarding data transmitted over the airwaves. These protocols, such as WEP, WPA, WPA2, and WPA3, are like locks guarding the digital gateways. Let's journey through each protocol, unravelling their intricacies.

WEP (Wired Equivalent Privacy): Back in the late 1990s, WEP emerged as an early attempt to mimic the security of wired networks in the wireless realm. It used the RC4 encryption algorithm, relying on a static key shared among devices. However, WEP quickly crumbled under scrutiny due to its vulnerabilities. Hackers could exploit weaknesses in the encryption mechanism, making WEP no more secure than an open door.

WPA (Wi-Fi Protected Access): With the realisation of WEP's shortcomings, WPA stepped onto the scene in 2003 as a temporary solution. It introduced dynamic encryption keys and a more robust integrity-checking mechanism. The use of TKIP improved security, but still, certain vulnerabilities persisted. WPA strived to bolster wireless security, but its design left room for attackers to find gaps in the armour.

WPA2 (Wi-Fi Protected Access 2): In 2004, the evolution continued with WPA2, the cornerstone of modern Wi-Fi security. AES-CCMP replaced TKIP, bringing robust encryption to the table. The 4-way handshake process established a secure connection, and strong, complex passwords became paramount. WPA2's fortress stood strong against most attacks, making it a preferred choice.

WPA3 (Wi-Fi Protected Access 3): Stepping into the present, WPA3 arrived in 2018, with even greater fortifications. Individualised data encryption became its hallmark, ensuring privacy even on open networks. Simultaneous Authentication of Equals (SAE) fought against offline dictionary attacks, rendering password guessing more difficult. WPA3's encryption remained steadfast, even on networks without passwords.

In this journey, the shift from WEP's fragile lock to WPA3's resilient fortress symbolises the relentless pursuit of wireless security. Each iteration, from WEP to WPA3, marks a stride forward—a response to threats, a commitment to defence. And so, in the complex landscape of wireless encryption protocols, the goal remains steadfast: to safeguard our digital highways, ensuring that data flows securely, and connections remain unbreakable.

Understanding Wireless Network Security: Peering Beyond the Signals

In the realm of wireless networks, the invisible signals that connect us carry more than just data—they transmit vulnerabilities and risks that can be exploited. Delving into the analysis of wireless network security becomes a crucial endeavour. It's akin to shining a light on the shadows, revealing the strategies that can fortify our digital frontiers.

Why Analyse Wireless Network Security? Wireless networks, by nature, emit signals that can be intercepted by anyone within range. This vulnerability underscores the importance of understanding the security mechanisms that protect these networks. Analysing wireless network security serves as a sentinel, guarding against potential breaches that could compromise data, personal information, and even privacy.

Exploring Concepts: SSID Broadcasting, MAC Filtering, and Hiding When analysing wireless network security, several key concepts come to the forefront:

1. SSID Broadcasting: Service Set Identifier (SSID) broadcasting is the practice of making the network's name visible to anyone within range. While it's convenient for users to identify and connect to networks, it also exposes the network to potential attackers who can use the SSID to gather information about the network.

2. MAC Filtering: Media Access Control (MAC) filtering involves restricting network access based on the MAC addresses of devices. While this can add a layer of security, attackers can spoof MAC addresses to bypass this filter.
3. Hiding Networks: Some networks opt to hide their SSID, making them non-discoverable. While this can provide a degree of obscurity, it's not foolproof and can still be detected by determined attackers.

Peering Behind the Curtain Through hands-on demonstrations, the theoretical concepts of wireless network security take on tangible form. As you interact with real-world scenarios, you'll uncover the subtleties that often evade theory alone.

Identifying Hidden Networks: Imagine a network that has chosen to hide its SSID, seeking a degree of security through obscurity. With hands-on experience, you'll delve into tools that can reveal these concealed networks, demonstrating the potential risks associated with their invisibility.

Assessing Vulnerabilities: In this exploratory journey, you'll not only uncover hidden networks but also assess their vulnerabilities. Through the eyes of an ethical hacker, you'll come to understand how attackers might exploit the perceived security of these networks. This exercise is not about encouraging intrusion, but rather about cultivating a proactive defence mentality.

Empowerment Through Knowledge: Analysing wireless network security isn't just about unveiling vulnerabilities—it's about empowerment. Armed with the insights gained through hands-on exploration, you become a guardian of your own digital space. You can make informed decisions about network settings, weigh the pros and cons of security measures, and, above all, contribute to a safer wireless landscape.

In the complex symphony of wireless signals, the harmony lies in understanding the intricacies of security measures. Through analysis and experimentation, you'll navigate the world of SSID broadcasting, MAC filtering, and hidden networks, emerging as a sentinel of wireless security—an individual capable of defending against the unseen threats that linger within the airwaves.

Performing Man-in-the-Middle Attacks on Wireless Networks: Wireless networks are susceptible to man-in-the-middle (MitM) attacks, where an attacker intercepts and alters communication between devices. We'll use tools like Ettercap to launch MitM attacks on wireless networks, intercepting and analysing traffic. You'll gain insights into the potential risks of unencrypted connections and learn mitigation strategies.

Hands-On Lab: Cracking WPA2 Passwords and Performing MitM Attack

Scenario: You'll be cracking a WPA2 password and performing a man-in-the-middle attack on a target wireless network.

Requirements:

- Kali Linux virtual machine (attacker)

- Access to a WPA2-protected wireless network (lab environment)

Steps:

1. **Cracking WPA2 Password:**
   - Use "airmon-ng" to put your wireless card into monitor mode.
   - Use "airodump-ng" to discover nearby wireless networks and capture handshake packets.
   - Launch a dictionary attack on the captured handshake using "aircrack-ng."
2. **Performing Man-in-the-Middle Attack:**
   - Use "airmon-ng" to enable monitor mode on your wireless card.
   - Use "airodump-ng" to identify target devices and capture traffic.
   - Use "Ettercap" to launch a MitM attack on the target device, intercepting its traffic.
3. **Analyse Intercepted Traffic:**
   - Use tools like Wireshark to analyse the intercepted traffic.
   - Observe the data being transmitted and understand the potential risks of unencrypted communication.

Ethical Considerations: Perform these activities in a controlled environment with explicit permission. Wireless network pentesting should be conducted responsibly and ethically.

Takeaways: By delving into Wireless Network Pentesting, you gain the ability to unveil the vulnerabilities hidden within the airwaves. This chapter empowers you to assess wireless security, crack passwords, and simulate man-in-the-middle attacks—ultimately contributing to the strengthening of digital defences against wireless threats.

Chapter 10: Social Engineering and Physical Security Testing - Unmasking the Human Element

In the realm of cybersecurity, where technology meets psychology, lies the art of Social Engineering and Physical Security Testing. This chapter delves into the intricate world of manipulating human behaviour and assessing the defences that protect the physical realm. Prepare to navigate the mindscape of deception and uncover vulnerabilities that extend beyond the digital landscape.

Understanding Social Engineering Tactics: Penetrating the Human Firewall

The most vulnerable link in any security chain is often the human element. We'll dive deep into social engineering tactics, where attackers leverage psychological manipulation to breach defences. Through real-world scenarios and case studies, you'll grasp the psychology behind pretexting, tailgating, baiting, and other social engineering techniques.

Conducting Phishing Campaigns: Crafting Digital Deception

Phishing is a prevalent attack vector, exploiting human trust and curiosity. You'll step into the shoes of an ethical hacker to craft and execute a controlled phishing campaign. With hands-on guidance, you'll learn how to create convincing phishing emails, design enticing lures, and use phishing tools to assess an organisation's susceptibility to such attacks.

Evaluating Physical Security Controls: Breaching the Tangible Barriers

While digital defences are paramount, the physical realm must not be overlooked. You'll gain insights into evaluating an organisation's physical security measures, from access controls to surveillance systems. Through simulated scenarios, you'll explore the art of tailgating, lock picking, and bypassing physical security controls to identify vulnerabilities that may compromise an organisation's overall security posture.

Hands-On Lab: Simulated Social Engineering and Physical Security Assessment

Scenario: You'll conduct a simulated social engineering and physical security assessment on a hypothetical organisation.

Requirements:

- Kali Linux virtual machine (attacker)
- Hypothetical organisation's physical location for the assessment

Steps:

1. **Understanding Social Engineering Tactics:**

- Study various social engineering techniques and their psychological underpinnings.
- Explore case studies to comprehend how real attacks exploit human psychology.

2. **Conducting Phishing Campaigns:**

- Craft a phishing email with a convincing pretext.

- Design an enticing lure to entice recipients into taking action.
- Utilise phishing tools (e.g., SET) to send the email and capture response data.

3. **Evaluating Physical Security Controls:**

- Survey the physical location and assess access controls.
- Simulate tailgating scenarios to test the effectiveness of access controls.
- Practice lock picking (if legally permissible) to explore vulnerabilities in physical locks.

By venturing into the realm of Social Engineering and Physical Security Testing, you become a guardian not only of technology but also of the human and tangible aspects of security. This chapter empowers you to understand the psychology behind manipulation, craft effective phishing campaigns, and assess the physical barriers that guard our digital landscapes.

Kali Linux Social-Engineer Toolkit (SET)

In the dimly lit realm of digital security, a powerful tool known as the Social-Engineer Toolkit (SET) emerges as a double-edged sword—a creation that can be harnessed for both ethical enlightenment and malicious manipulation. As we venture into the depths of this toolkit, we find ourselves at a crossroads where knowledge meets responsibility.

The SET Prologue: A Menu of Possibilities

With a keystroke, the terminal unveils the SET menu, a sprawling landscape of choices that promise to unlock the secrets of human psychology and digital vulnerability. Each option is a gateway to a different chapter in the story, shaping the narrative of ethical exploration or malevolent intent.

1. Social-Engineering Attacks: The first choice leads to the realm of social engineering, a territory where the manipulation of human behaviour becomes a powerful weapon. With each selection within this realm, the lines between empathy and deception blur. Pretexting, a guise that deceives the mind, stands as a door to gaining trust. Baiting, a digital temptation, lures unsuspecting souls into dangerous territories. Every choice in this path showcases the fine line between a genuine connection and a digital trap.

2. Credential Harvester Attack Method: The credential harvester—an apt metaphor for a modern-day hunter—sets its sights on capturing precious digital trophies: usernames and passwords. The terrain is littered with cloned websites that tempt victims to enter their secrets. The attacker's lair—guarded by a Java applet attack—lures them in with promises of security. The harvester cunningly captures what it seeks, a reminder that even in the virtual world, trust can lead to vulnerability.

3. Manually Create a Payload: In a world where code can dance on the edge of morality, the option to create payloads emerges. Each payload is like a spell, a snippet of malicious code that holds the potential to exploit vulnerabilities. The heart races as the attacker crafts this digital enchantment,

knowing that once unleashed, it holds the power to breach defences.

4. Update the Social-Engineer Toolkit: Here, the tools evolve—a reminder that the digital world never stands still. In the constant battle between defenders and attackers, staying up to date becomes a necessity. The choice to update is a symbol of the relentless pursuit of knowledge, an acknowledgment that security is a journey, not a destination.

5. Return to the Main Menu: A return to the beginning—a sanctuary from the ethereal journey. This choice signifies the breath between actions, a moment to reflect on the path chosen and the intentions behind it.

6. Help, Credits, and About: In a world shrouded in enigma, the guidebook stands as a beacon. The Help option offers a map, providing clarity in a realm of complexity. The Credits reveal the architects behind the curtain, the minds that conceived this digital labyrinth. About—here, the essence of SET is distilled, and the purpose crystallises.

As we navigate the labyrinth of options, we are confronted with a choice—to wield this toolkit as a force for good, an instrument of enlightenment, or to harness it with malice, exploiting the vulnerabilities it unveils. Each choice, a chapter in a tale of ethics and responsibility, shapes the narrative of cybersecurity—a narrative that carries the weight of a digital age seeking balance between knowledge and morality.

Hands on: Social Engineering with the Social-Engineer Toolkit (SET)

Objective: To perform a simulated social engineering attack using SET in Kali Linux.

Requirements:

- Kali Linux virtual machine
- A target email address (use your own or a controlled environment for ethical purposes)

Steps:

Step 1: Launch Kali Linux

- Start your Kali Linux virtual machine.

Step 2: Open a Terminal

- Click on the terminal icon or press Ctrl + Alt + T to open a terminal window.

Step 3: Launch the Social-Engineer Toolkit (SET)

- In the terminal, type the following command to launch SET:

    setoolkit

Step 4: Welcome Screen

- You will be greeted with the SET menu. Type 1 to select "Social-Engineering Attacks."

Step 5: Choose the Attack Vector

- Type 2 to select "Website Attack Vectors."

Step 6: Choose the Credential Harvester Attack

- Type 3 to choose "Credential Harvester Attack Method."

Step 7: Set the IP Address

- SET will ask you for your IP address. Enter your Kali Linux machine's IP address. You can find it by typing ifconfig in another terminal window.

Step 8: Set the Port

- SET will ask you for the port to listen on. You can leave it as the default (80) and press Enter.

Step 9: Set the Site to Clone

- You will be prompted to enter the URL of the site you want to clone (usually a login page). Enter a website URL that you control or have permission to test against.

Step 10: Enable the Java Applet Attack

- Type Y to enable the Java Applet attack. This increases the chances of capturing credentials.

Step 11: Generate the Attack

- SET will generate a fake login page for the website you specified.

Step 12: Start the Web Server

- SET will ask you if you want to start the Apache web server. Type Y to start the web server.

Step 13: Wait for Credentials

- SET will wait for users to visit the fake login page. When someone enters their credentials, SET will capture them and display them in the terminal.

Step 14: Review Captured Credentials

- As credentials are captured, they will be displayed on the screen. Take note of any usernames and passwords that are captured.

Step 15: Stop the Attack

- To stop the attack, press Ctrl + C in the terminal where SET is running.

Step 16: Clean Up

- To clean up the attack, type 5 to return to the main menu, and then type 2 to select "Teardown Attacks." Follow the prompts to tear down the attack.

Ethical Considerations:

- This lab is for educational purposes only and should only be conducted in controlled environments with proper authorisation.
- Do not use SET or any social engineering techniques for malicious purposes.

Note: Social engineering attacks like these are illegal if conducted without proper authorisation. Always adhere to ethical guidelines and obtain permission before conducting any security testing or assessment.

Navigating the Complex Terrain of Social Engineering

In the labyrinth of cybersecurity, social engineering stands as a challenge that transcends code and hardware. It is a battle fought in the realm of psychology, where human vulnerabilities are exploited to breach digital defences. As we stand at the crossroads of knowledge and deception, the challenges posed by social engineering demand our unwavering attention and action.

The intricacies of human behaviour present an ever-shifting landscape for attackers to navigate. Trust, curiosity, and fear are emotions skilfully manipulated to extract sensitive information or coax individuals into dangerous actions.

Social engineering tactics are not stagnant. They adapt, evolve, and morph with each new innovation in technology. Attackers are quick to adopt novel methods, making it challenging for defenders to predict and counteract their moves.

Insiders, with their knowledge of an organisation's processes and people, can pose a grave risk. From disgruntled employees to well-intentioned but misguided staff, the human factor can lead to breaches that technology alone cannot prevent.

Mitigations and Strategies:

Education and Awareness: Training staff to recognise social engineering tactics is paramount. Simulated phishing campaigns and interactive workshops help individuals develop a sense of scepticism and the ability to identify suspicious communications.

Strong Authentication Mechanisms: Requiring multi-factor authentication adds an extra layer of security, even if an attacker manages to obtain credentials through social engineering. It makes unauthorised access considerably more difficult.

Monitoring and Incident Response: Employing advanced monitoring tools allows organisations to detect unusual behaviour promptly. Incident response plans must be in place to quickly address breaches and mitigate their impact.

Regular Security Audits: Conducting regular security audits evaluates the organisation's vulnerabilities, including those stemming from social engineering. By identifying weak points, defenders can reinforce their lines of defence.

Policy and Procedures: Enforcing strict security policies and procedures establishes guidelines for employees to follow. Additionally, implementing clear protocols for handling sensitive information reduces the risk of inadvertent exposure.

Conclusion:

Social engineering is a complex adversary, wielding the power to exploit human psychology and breach the most fortified digital walls. It calls for a holistic approach—one that combines technology, education, and vigilance. As we navigate the digital realm, we must be mindful of our vulnerabilities and steadfast in our efforts to protect against the snares of manipulation. By staying informed, fostering a culture of security awareness, and embracing best practices, we can fortify ourselves against the intricate challenges posed by social engineering. In this battle of wits and ethics, knowledge is our shield, and responsibility our guiding light.

Chapter 11: Reporting and documentation

In the world of ethical hacking and penetration testing, the journey isn't complete until the insights gained are translated into actionable information. This crucial phase, encapsulated in the realm of Reporting and Documentation, serves as the bridge between discovery and resolution—a testament to professionalism, thoroughness, and the ethical commitment to safeguarding digital landscapes.

Documenting Findings and Vulnerabilities: The Language of Insights

As the digital detective, armed with tools and knowledge, you navigate the digital labyrinth, uncovering vulnerabilities that might otherwise go unnoticed. But the true value of your findings lies not just in their discovery but in their meticulous documentation. This documentation paints a vivid picture, capturing the vulnerabilities' essence, their potential consequences, and the avenues through which they were unearthed.

Here, industry standards such as the Common Vulnerability Scoring System (CVSS) come into play, providing a structured framework to assess the severity of vulnerabilities. Each CVSS score speaks volumes, conveying the risk's magnitude and guiding the prioritisation of remediation efforts. The documentation becomes a tapestry, woven with details— CVE identifiers, exploitability assessments, and potential attack vectors—offering a comprehensive snapshot for those who will act upon your insights.

Moreover, the nature of documentation might vary based on global regulations and laws. Countries have different data protection and privacy regulations that impact how and what kind of data can be documented. Understanding these regulations, such as the European Union's General Data Protection Regulation (GDPR) or the Health Insurance Portability and Accountability Act (HIPAA) in the United States, is essential to ensure that your documentation complies with legal requirements.

Crafting Effective Pentest Reports: The Art of Clarity

In a world where digital jargon can be as dense as a thicket, the pentest report emerges as an instrument of clarity. It is not just a recitation of vulnerabilities; it's a narrative that elucidates, educates, and empowers. The report's structure becomes paramount, following industry standards like the Penetration Testing Execution Standard (PTES) or ISO/IEC 27001.

The narrative weaves through the scope of the assessment, the methodology employed, the findings discovered, and their potential impact. Vulnerabilities are laid bare, supported by evidence and context, guiding defenders on the path to mitigation. Severity assessments—often aligned with standards like CVSS—enable stakeholders to gauge the urgency and allocate resources appropriately.

Communicating Technical Details to Non-Technical Stakeholders: The Art of Translation

In a realm where technical prowess reigns, the challenge arises when the audience extends beyond the realm of the technically adept. Here, the art of translation flourishes—a delicate dance of conveying complexity in a language understood by all.

Aided by visual aids—graphs, charts, and tables—the technical details morph into meaningful insights. The report morphs from a code-laden manuscript into an accessible narrative that empowers decision-makers to grasp the risks and make informed choices. It's an art that takes the diverse language of cybersecurity and renders it universally comprehensible.

In conclusion, Reporting and Documentation is more than a postscript—it's the culmination of ethical hacking's purpose. It's the translation of discoveries into actions, the articulation of vulnerabilities into safeguards, and the synthesis of complexity into understanding. As you navigate this phase, remember that the tale you tell through your reports is a powerful catalyst for change—a clarion call to fortify, rectify, and protect the digital realms we inhabit, while also respecting the unique regulatory landscapes that shape our global interconnectedness.

Chapter 12: Continuous Learning and Career Pathways - Navigating the Dynamic Seas of Cybersecurity

In the ever-shifting landscape of cybersecurity, the journey is not just about arriving at a destination—it's about embracing a perpetual expedition of learning, growth, and professional evolution. This chapter delves into the realm of Continuous Learning and Career Pathways, illuminating the vital importance of staying informed, pursuing certifications, understanding the basics of networking and operating systems, and exploring the diverse avenues that the cybersecurity domain offers.

Staying Up-to-Date with Evolving Threats: The Unceasing Odyssey

In the digital age, where innovation races at breakneck speed, threats evolve in tandem. Herein lies the challenge—to remain relevant and vigilant in the face of ever-adapting adversaries. Staying updated is not just a choice; it's a necessity. With the emergence of new attack vectors, malware strains, and vulnerabilities, continuous learning becomes a safeguard against obsolescence.

Pursuing Certifications: Forging Credentials of Expertise

Certifications stand as digital badges of honour—testaments to your expertise, commitment, and depth of knowledge. They not only enhance your credibility but also broaden your skillset. The Certified Ethical Hacker (CEH) certification validates your ability to think and act like a hacker, enabling you to anticipate their tactics. The Offensive Security

Certified Professional (OSCP) challenges you to prove your hands-on skills through intense real-world scenarios.

Understanding the Basics: The Foundation of Expertise

In the realm of cybersecurity, understanding the basics is akin to constructing a solid foundation before erecting a skyscraper. Knowledge of networking fundamentals—TCP/IP, subnetting, and protocols—provides you with the context to decipher the intricacies of cyber threats. Similarly, grasping the architecture and vulnerabilities of operating systems arms you with the insight to detect and counteract potential breaches.

Exploring Career Opportunities in Cybersecurity: Navigating the Cyber Cosmos

Cybersecurity is not a monolithic entity; it's a sprawling galaxy of roles, each with its unique orbit and purpose. From becoming a Penetration Tester who actively seeks vulnerabilities to a Security Analyst who monitors and mitigates threats, the career paths in cybersecurity are as diverse as they are rewarding.

- **Penetration Tester:** Unearth vulnerabilities in digital fortresses, leveraging your skills to expose weaknesses and empower organisations to fortify their defences.
- **Security Analyst:** Keep a watchful eye on network activities, identifying and neutralising threats as they emerge, ensuring the digital realm remains secure.

- **Incident Responder:** In the aftermath of breaches, step into action, mitigating damage, restoring systems, and ensuring a swift return to normalcy.
- **Security Consultant:** Provide expert guidance, helping organisations identify vulnerabilities and devise strategies to safeguard their digital assets.
- **Cybersecurity Manager:** Oversee the orchestration of security measures, from policy creation to crisis management, ensuring the organisation's digital posture remains robust.

Conclusion: Embarking on a Lifelong Quest

As the digital frontier expands, the need for cybersecurity warriors intensifies. The journey doesn't conclude with a single certification or a solitary role—it's an odyssey of continuous learning, of embracing new certifications, of understanding the foundational principles, and of exploring diverse career opportunities. In a world defined by bytes and data, your role as a guardian of digital integrity evolves with each threat that emerges.

Embrace the ethos of lifelong learning, let certifications bolster your expertise, understand the basics to fortify your foundation, and explore the myriad pathways that cybersecurity unveils. In doing so, you become an indomitable force—a sentry of the digital realm, unyielding in your commitment to protect, defend, and navigate the ever-evolving seas of cyberspace.

Useful Linux Commands

Some useful Linux commands that can be valuable for various tasks, including system administration, troubleshooting, file management, and more:

1. **Navigating and Listing Files:**
   o ls: List files and directories.
   o cd: Change the current directory.
   o pwd: Print the current working directory.
   o mkdir: Create a new directory.
   o rm: Remove files or directories.
   o cp: Copy files or directories.
   o mv: Move or rename files or directories.
2. **File and Text Manipulation:**
   o cat: Display the contents of a file.
   o grep: Search for specific patterns in files.
   o echo: Print text to the terminal.
   o nano or vim: Text editors for creating or editing files.
   o chmod: Change file permissions.
   o chown: Change file ownership.
3. **System Information and Monitoring:**
   o top: Display real-time system resource usage.
   o df: Show disk space usage.
   o du: Display file and directory space usage.
   o ps: List running processes.
   o free: Display memory usage.
   o uptime: Show system uptime.
4. **Networking:**
   o ifconfig or ip: Display network interface information.

- ping: Send ICMP echo requests to test network connectivity.
- netstat: Show network statistics.
- ss: Display socket statistics.
- nc: Netcat utility for network communication.

5. **Package Management:**
   - apt or apt-get: Package management tool for Debian-based systems.
   - yum: Package management tool for Red Hat-based systems.
   - pacman: Package management tool for Arch Linux.

6. **User and Group Management:**
   - useradd: Add a new user.
   - passwd: Change user password.
   - usermod: Modify user properties.
   - groupadd: Add a new group.
   - sudo: Execute commands as another user (often root).

7. **Processes and Job Control:**
   - ps: List processes.
   - kill: Terminate processes.
   - bg: Run a suspended process in the background.
   - fg: Bring a background process to the foreground.
   - jobs: List background jobs.

8. **Archiving and Compression:**
   - tar: Create, extract, or manipulate tar archives.
   - gzip or gunzip: Compress or decompress files.

- zip or unzip: Create, extract, or manipulate zip archives.

These commands provide a foundation for performing a wide range of tasks on a Linux system. Remember to consult the manual (man command) for detailed information about each command and its usage.

References

1. Erickson, J. (2008). Hacking: The Art of Exploitation. No Starch Press.
2. Stuttard, D., & Pinto, M. (2011). The Web Application Hacker's Handbook: Finding and Exploiting Security Flaws. Wiley.
3. Kennedy, D., O'Gorman, J., Kearns, D., & Aharoni, M. (2011). Metasploit: The Penetration Tester's Guide. No Starch Press.
4. Engebretson, P. (2013). The Basics of Hacking and Penetration Testing: Ethical Hacking and Penetration Testing Made Easy. Syngress.
5. Walker, M. (2019). CEH Certified Ethical Hacker All-in-One Exam Guide. McGraw-Hill Education.
6. Kim, P. (2018). The Hacker Playbook 3: Practical Guide To Penetration Testing. Independently published.
7. Sikorski, M., & Honig, A. (2012). Practical Malware Analysis: A Hands-On Guide to Dissecting Malicious Software. No Starch Press.
8. Chappell, L., & Combs, G. (2010). Wireshark Network Analysis (Second Edition): The Official Wireshark

Certified Network Analyst Study Guide. Laura
Chappell University.

9. Hertzog, R., O'Gorman, J., & Aharoni, M. (2017). Kali
    Linux Revealed: Mastering the Penetration Testing
    Distribution. Offsec Press.
10. Weidman, G. (2016). Penetration Testing: A Hands-
    On Introduction to Hacking. No Starch Press.
11. Yaworski, P. (2018). Web Hacking 101: How to Make
    Money Hacking Ethically. LeanPub.
12. OWASP Top Ten Project. (https://owasp.org/www-
    project-top-ten/)
13. Nmap Official Website. (https://nmap.org/)
14. Shodan. (https://www.shodan.io/)
15. OpenVAS. (https://www.openvas.org/)
16. Burp Suite Official Website.
    (https://portswigger.net/burp)
17. Official OWASP Website. (https://owasp.org/)
18. ISO/IEC 27001: Information security management
    systems - Requirements.
    (https://www.iso.org/standard/54534.html)
19. Common Vulnerability Scoring System (CVSS)
    Documentation. (https://www.first.org/cvss/)
20. Penetration Testing Execution Standard (PTES).
    (http://www.pentest-standard.org/)
21. European Union General Data Protection Regulation
    (GDPR). (https://gdpr-info.eu/)
22. Health Insurance Portability and Accountability Act
    (HIPAA). (https://www.hhs.gov/hipaa/)
23. Offensive Security Certified Professional (OSCP)
    Certification. (https://www.offensive-
    security.com/pwk-oscp/)

24. Certified Ethical Hacker (CEH) Certification. (https://www.eccouncil.org/programs/certified-ethical-hacker-ceh/)